호모 로퀜스 정체 밝히기

언어와 정보사회 학술 총서 04

호모 로퀜스Homo loquens
정체 밝히기

김형민·신승용·정수정·김광섭·연재훈·김지영

역락

간행사

언어는 자연물로 존재하는 동시에 역사성과 사회성도 띤다. 따라서 언어의 정체를 온전히 밝히려면 자연물로서의 언어를 탐구하는 과학적 자세와 더불어 역사적, 사회적 존재로서의 언어를 이해하기 위한 인문학적, 사회학적 자세도 필요하다. 이러한 관점에서 서강대학교 언어정보연구소는 인간의 언어를 이해하기 위해 다양한 학술 활동을 기획하여 실행해 오고 있다. "『언어와 정보사회』 학술 총서"는 등재 학술지 『언어와 정보사회』와 상호보완적이며, 특히 짧은 논문에 담기 어려운 긴 호흡과 깊은 통찰을 필요로 하는 연구에 초점을 맞춘다. 이 총서를 통해 지금까지의 연구가 노정하고 있는 한계를 넘어서 새로운 이해의 지평이 개척되길 희망한다.

서강대학교 언어정보연구소

언어는 인간에게 우연이기보다는 필연이다. 인간의 언어 능력은 직립 보행 능력, 도구 사용 능력, 사유 능력 등과 함께 인간의 가장 본질적인 속성에 속한다. 그래서 인간의 '인간됨'을 잘 보여주는 것이 언어이다.

언어학자의 관점에서 바라보면 호모 사피엔스(homo sapiens)는 특히 호모 로퀜스(homo loquens)이다. 이때 homo sapiens의 자구적 의미는 '이성적인 인간, 슬기로운 인간, 사유하는 인간'이며, homo loquens의 자구적 의미는 '말하는 인간'이다. 호모 사피엔스는 다른 사람에게 말을 건네고, 다른 사람의 말을 듣는데 평생 동안 많은 시간을 소비한다. 호모 사피엔스는 언어와 떼려야 뗄 수 없는 불가분의 관계를 맺고 있다. 그래서 호모 사피엔스의 가장 두드러진 특징 중 하나가 바로 호모 로퀜스적 속성이다.

언어학의 핵심 과제 중 하나, 다시 말해 언어학자의 핵심 목표 중 하나는 호모 로퀜스의 언어 능력을 규명하는 일일 수 있다. '호모 로퀜스의 언어 능력'은 실질적으로 '호모 로퀜스의 정체'이다. 따라서 '호모 로퀜스의 정체 밝히기'가 언어학의 핵심 과제이자 언어학자의 핵심 목표일 수 있다.

서강대학교 언어정보연구소의 '언어와 정보사회 학술 총서 4'는 호모 로퀜스의 정체를 밝히기 위한 노력의 일환으로 기획되었다. 이런 노력은 '진행형'으로 앞으로도 지속적으로 행해질 것이다. 여기저기 흩어져 있는 꿈을 모아 희망을 만들 수 있듯이, 작은 노력을 모아 소기의 목적에 도달할 수 있기를 기대해 본다.

2022년 3월
서강대학교 언어정보연구소 소장 김형민

차례

Der Einfluss des *i*-Umlauts auf die morphologischen Ebene im Altenglischen

Hyeong Min Kim

1. Einleitende Bemerkungen

Seit langer Zeit ist es schon selbstverständlich, dass sich alle lebendigen Sprachen mit der Zeit verändert haben, verändern und verändern werden. Mit dieser allgemein anerkannten Tatsache steht eine Frage im engeren Zusammenhang: Warum wandeln sich Sprachen? Als Ursachen des Sprachwandels können in der Tat die sprachsysteminternen und die sprachsystemexternen Faktoren angeführt werden. Bei den ersteren handelt es sich hauptsächlich um die innerlinguistischen Faktoren, die systembedingten Veränderungen und die inneren Umgestaltungen in der Sprache, die in Wahrheit dem Ökonomieprinzip und dem Differenziertheitsprinzip folgen sollten. Bei den letzteren geht es dagegen um die extralinguistischen Faktoren, die z.B. durch die psychologischen und/oder physischen Bedingungen der Sprechenden und/oder die sie umschließende Umwelt usw. bewirkt werden[1] (vgl. Allgemeine Sprachwissenschaft 1973, 183ff.; Linke & Nussbaumer & Portmann 1996, 378f.). Gleichgültig, welche Faktoren bzw. Ursachen überhaupt den Sprachwandel vorantreiben, kann man die Veränderung der Sprache in verschiedenen linguistischen Mikro- und Makroebenen - der phonetischen, phonologischen, morphologischen, syntaktischen, lexikologischen, wortbildenden, semantischen, pragmatischen u.a.m. - feststellen, z.B. mit Hilfe von Vergleich zwischen dem früheren Sprachzustand und dem späteren und sogar zwischen Generationen in demselben Zeitalter.

Wie viele andere sprachliche Erscheinungen - z.B. grammatischer Wechsel, Ablaut etc. - spielt die Umlautung, besonders der i-Umlaut, in der Entwicklung einer Sprache, vor allem des Englischen und des Deutschen, eine entscheidende Rolle. Unter vielen den beträchtlichen Sprachwandel verursachenden lautlichen Phänomenen ereignet sich diese Mutationserscheinung relativ früh - wenn auch in den einzelnen Sprachen unterschiedlich - und übt auch den bedeutsamen Einfluss auf verschiedene Sprachebenen im engeren Sinne aus, nämlich die sprachlichen Mikrostrukturen wie die phonetische, phonologische, morphologische, wortbildende Ebene usw.[2] In die ganze Geschichte einer Sprache zurückgeblickt, kann man daraus folgern, dass der Wandel eines sprachlichen Phänomens entweder durch die

---

1   Als weitere Motivationen zur Sprachverändernug können auch die mehr oder weniger einseitigen Einflüsse der einen Sprache auf die andere und die gegenseitig bedingten Sprachkontaktphänomene angesehen werden.

2   Zu einer detaillierten Beschreibung des Einflusses des i-Umlauts auf wortbildende Sprachebenen im Altenglischen, vgl. Kim 2006.

inneren oder die äußeren Bedingungen bzw. Ursachen oder durch die beiden hervorgerufen worden ist. In keinem Fall beschränkte sich dieser Wandel auf eine singuläre Wirkung, sondern setzt bei seiner Verbreitung eine Reihe von weiteren Folgen in Bewegung. Das gilt auch für die Umlautung, insbesondere den *i*-Umlaut.

Das Ziel der vorliegenden Arbeit besteht darin, den Einfluss des *i*-Umlauts auf die morphologische Ebene im Altenglischen zu analysieren und darzustellen. Dadurch wird versucht, die Gesetzmäßigkeiten der morphologisch bedingten Umlautung (bzw. des morphologischen Umlauts) festzustellen.

2. Bestimmung des Umlauts

Die Geschichte einer Sprache lehrt uns, dass sowohl das kanonisierende bzw. standardisierende Schriftsystem als auch die Entwicklung der Massenmedien und dergleichen zumindest die Geschwindigkeit der Sprachveränderung, abstrahiert von der lexikalischen Ebene, in gewissem Grade gegenüber den älteren Sprachstufen vermindern können. Trotzdem verwandeln sich die Sprachen unablässig und unaufhörlich, insofern sie lebendig verwendet werden, unabhängig davon, dass wir die relativ konservativen und in der Regel der Norm nach festgesetzten Schriftzeichen besitzen oder nicht. Im Anschluss an den Gebrauch einer Sprache kann man also sagen, die Sprache müsse „gewissermaßen die Kräfte zu ihrer eigenen Überwindung, zum sog.

Sprachwandel, schon in sich tragen" (Coseriu 1975, 138).

Für die Erklärung des Umlauts sind also nicht nur die älteren schriftichen Aufzeichnungen und die Schreibungen der verwandten Sprachen zu berücksichtigen, sondern auch die zu rekonstruierenden Ursprachen, von denen es keine schrifltichen Dokumente gibt, denn in vielen Fällen der überlieferten ältersten Texte selbst - in den meisten aus dem idg. Ursprache stammenden Sprachen - sind die umlautbewirkenden Faktoren nicht mehr zu erkennen. Bevor die Abgrenzung bzw. Begriffsbestimmung der Umlauterscheinung vorgenommen wird, ist es wahrscheinlich aufschlussreich, in erster Linie von allgemeinen Typen des Lautwandels zu sprechen. Dadurch lässt sich der Stellenwert des Umlauts im Lautwandel wie im Sprachwandel noch eindeutiger ermitteln.

Basieren darauf, dass jeder abstrakte Lauteinheit, noch genauer jedes Phonem, im Bereich der Parole mit einigen Varianten realisiert werden kann, dass jeder konkrete Laut mit den anderen im Kontinuum nebeneinander steht und dass lautliche Neuerungen nach und nach nur in einer bestimmten Sprachgemeinschaft die Durchsetzungskraft gewinnen können, lassen sich die Typen des Lautwandels einteilen[3](vgl. Görlach 1982, 48; Schweikle 1987, Weimann 1982, 64-68):

(1) spontaner Lautwandel (d.h. Lautveränderung unabhänig von lautlichen

---

3   G. Schweikle teilte den von bestimmter lautlicher Atmosphäre abhängigen Lautwandel noch weitgehend in kombinatorischen Lautwandel im engeren Sinne (z.B. Umlaut), akzentbedingten (z.B. der Vernersches Gesetz) und stellungsbedinten Lautwandel (z.B. Auslautverhärtung).

Umgebungen, z.B. die erste Lautverschiebung, Rhotazismus etc.);

(2) kombinatorischer Lautwandel (d.i. Lautwandlung angewiesen auf bestimmte lautliche Umgebungen, z.B. Umlaut, Assimilation, das Vernersche Gesetz, Auslautverhärtung etc.);

(3) sporadischer Lautwandel (nämlich, Lautwechsel gebunden an bestimmte Zeichen in einzelnen Wörtern, z.B. Metathese etc.).[4]

Durch den Umlaut erfolgt die qualitative Umwandlung eines Vokals in der Stammsilbe, wobei die lautliche Umgebung, die Qualität eines Vokals bzw. Halbvokals in der folgenden Silbe, als ein solche Änderung induzierendes Moment fungiert. Daher wird der Umlaut also als vokalische Qualitätsveränderung und kombinatorischer Lautwandel betrachtet. Darüber hinaus gehört das Umlautphänomen zur Assimilation, in der sich Laut „an andere Laute des Sprachkontinuums durch Anpassung der Artikulationsbewegungen"

---

4   Diese Typen der Lautveränderungen fußen auf einem dem Sprechenden bzw. Hörenden vielleicht unbewussten und graduellen Sprachwandel. In Bezug auf die Bewusstseinsstufe zeigt H. Scheuringer (1992, 484ff.) im Rahmen der Dialektologie eine andere Klassifizierungsmöglichkeit des Lautwandels auf. In Anschluss an E. Kranzmayer (1956, 9 u. 17) nimmt er „eine für die Wiener [dialektologische: KHM] Schule typische Dichotomie" (E. Seidelmann 1987, 202), *echten Lautwandel* und *Lautersatz*, an. Während es beim Ersteren (z.B. Lautverschiebung) und Merkmale des Unbewussten, Ausnahmslosen, Gesetzmäßigen und Internbedingten geht, handelt es sich beim Letzteren (z.B. die angestrebte Beseitigung lautlicher Kontraste zu als höherwertig angesehenen Sprachformen) um Mermale des Bewussten, Ausnahmshaften, soziologische Gebundenen und Externbedingten. Zu diesen beiden fügt er eine dritte Möglichkeit des Lautwandels (z.B. Entnasalisierung auslautender Nasalvokale in den Stadtgebieten München und Wien) hinzu, bei dem Merkmale des Unbewussten, Ausnahmslosen, Graduellen und extralinguistisch Bedingten eine relevante Rolle spielt. Dieser Lautwandel wird als *Lautwandel durch äußere Kausalität* (Terminus von H. Scheuringer) oder *adaptiver Lautwandel* (Terminus von E. Seidelmann) bezeichnet.

(Lewandowski 1990, 98) angleichen. Dabei handelt es sich hauptsächlich um artikulatorische Erleichterung, wenn selbst in der heutigen Bestandnahme des Umlauts der Grund dafür nicht mehr zu finden ist.

2.1. Zum Begriff des Umlauts

Mit Umlaut werden diejenigen qualitativen Veränderungen eines betonten Stammvokals bezeichnet, welche durch einen Vokal in der Folgesilbe bewirkt werden. Dabei handelt es sich um die teilweise oder völlige Assimilation eines Vokals an einen Vokal in der folgenden Silbe[5] (vgl. Benett 1969, 7).

(1) germ. *full-ijan- > ae. *fyllan* > ne. *fill* 'füllen'

   ahd. *wurfil* > mhd. *würfel* 'Würfel'

Germ. *full-ijan-* und ahd. *wurfil* werden durch *i*-Umlaut jeweils zu ae. *fyllan* und mhd. *würfel*. Die akzenttragenden Stammvokale [*u] und [u] verändern sich also dem folgenden [i] gemäß zu [y] <ü>. Dabei geht es um den durch eine bestimmte lautliche Umgebung hervorgerufenen kombinatorischen Lautwandel, den sich vom hohen, hinteren und gerundeten zum hohen, vorderen und gerundeten Vokal verändernden

---

5 Bennett(1969, 7) schreibt, „Umlaut is a change in quality of accented radical vowel by a sound in the following syllable. In reality, it is an attempt to accommodate the quality of a proceeding sound to that of a sound which follows."

qualitativen Vokalwechsel, nämlich Palatalisierung, und die teilweise regressive Assimilation des vorhergehenden Vokals an den vorderen Vokal in der Folgensilbe.

2.2. Typologie des Umlautsphänomens

Je nach der Art des umlauterzeugenden Lautes kann eine Typologie des Umlautphänomens erscheinen: *i*-Umlaut, *u*-Umlaut, *o/a*-Umlaut. Die letzten beiden lassen sich zusammen als Velarumlaut benennen, weil der Einfluss des [u] und [o]/[a] in der folgenden Silbe auf den vorhergehenden Stammsilbevokal gleich ist[6](vgl. Luick 1921, 202f.; Brunner 1965, 68).

2.2.1. *i*-Umlaut

Durch den Einfluss des /i, ī, j/ in der Folgesilbe können die vorhergehenden Hinterzungenvokale in Richtung Kardinalvokal [i] verschoben werden. Dabei spricht man von *i*-Umlaut, der sich von Ablaut unterscheiden muss, weil unter Ablaut diejenigen qualitativen oder quantitativen Vokalveränderungen in verwandten Wörtern und Wortteilen verstanden werden, welche unter Bewahrung des konsonantischen Skeletts des Stamms von der lautlichen Umgebung unabhängig sind[7](vgl. Bammesberger 1984a 38 u. 46).

----

6   K. Brunner(1965, 68, Anm. 2) sagt: „Die Zusammenfassung des *a/o*- und des *u*-Umlauts als Verlarumlaut stamme von K. Luick. ... Die praktische einheitliche Bezeichnung Luicks habe sich seither [im Jahre 1914, als das Buch von Luick zuerst erschien: KHM] in der ae. grammatischen Literatur weitgehend durchgesetzt ...“

Eine der hervorstechendsten und für die germanischen verwandten Sprachen charakteristischen lautlichen Neuerungen ist der *i*-Umlaut, der aber in den einzelnen Sprachen in puncto ihrer individuellen Eigenschaften hinsichtlich des lautlichen, morphologischen und grammatischen Systems mehr oder weniger unterschiedlich geschieht.

In der Entwicklung des Englischen nimmt der *i*-Umlaut einen beträchtlichen Einfluss auf die phonologische, morphologische und lexikalische Struktur des Altenglischen ein. Bis jetzt kommt jedoch keine beweisbare Aussage über die Datierung des *i*-Umlaut vor. Es wird nur angenommen, dass im Englischen der *i*-Umlaut aus dem 6. Jahrhundert, der Periode des Uraltenglischen.,[8] datiert(vgl. Pinsker 1974, 22). Im Laufe der weiteren Sprachentwicklung zum Altenglischen hin, wird das umlautbewirkende /i/ schon zu /ə/ abgeschwächt und ist der umlauterzeugende Halbvokal /j/ meist ganz geschwunden(vgl. Faiß 1989, 27). In den ältesten ae. Schreibungen selbst, die aus der Zeit um 700 stammen, zeigen sich in meisten Fällen keine Umlautauslöser. Für die Feststellung des *i*-Umlauts sind deswegen auch von großer Wichtigkeit die jüngeren und älteren Texte verwandter Sprachen als Altenglischen, und zwar Althochdeutschen, Altnordisch, Gotisch und so fort.

---

7   Ablaut ist „ursprünglich eine rein phonetisch-phonologische Erscheinung" (Bußmann 2002, 44), die durch Stellung und Art des Akzents bedingt entstand. Vokalwechsel dieser Art wurde jedoch schon im Idg. morphologisiert, indem der Ablaut vorwiegend zur Tempusbildung der starken Verben und in der Wortbildung verwendet wurde: z.B. nhd. binden – band – gebunden (in den Stammformen der starken Verben); nhd. sprechen – Sprache – Spruch (in den Wortbildungsprozessen).

8   Unter Periode des Uraltenglischen verstehen wir die Zeit zwischen der germanischen Invasion nach England und dem ersten Auftreten der schriftlich ererbten Literatur.

Im Altenglischen erfasst der *i*-Umlaut eine Reihe von Lauten:

I. *i*-Umlaut der Monophthonge

1. *a(:)* > *æ(:)*

(2) germ. **aski-* > ae. *æsc* 'Esche'

    ae. *faran* 'fahren' ae. *færes(t)* 'du fährst' (< germ. **far-is*[9])

    vlat. **ladino* > ae. *læden* 'Latein'

    ae. *hāl* 'Heil' ae. *hǣlan* 'heilen' (< got. *hailjan*[10])

2. *a* > *e*

(3) ae. *lang* (< germ. **langa-*) 'lang'

    ae. *lengra* (< germ. **lang-izan-*[11]) 'länger'

    wg. **sattjan* > ae. *settan* 'setzen'

---

9   Germ. **-is* ist die verbale Endung der 2. Person Präsens Indikativ, wodurch der *i*-Umlaut auftritt.

10   Got. *hailjan* entwickelt sich durch die Aufhellung, die für Altenglisch und Altfriesisch charakteristisch ist, zu **hāljon* (aisl. /ai/ > /ā/, z.B. got. *stains*, ahd. *stein*, ae. *stān*; /a/ > /a:/, z.B. germ. **langa-*, ahd. *lang*, *lanc*, ae. *lang*, afrz. *lang, long*) (vgl. Bammesberger 1989, 68; Pinsker 1974, 19f.)

11   Bei der Umwandlung der komparativen Endung germ. **-izan* > ae. *-ra* handelt es sich um einen spontanen Wandel von germ. [z] in der intervokalischen Position zu wg. [r], der als Rhotazismus bezeichnet wird (vgl. Bammesberger 1989, 67; Bußmann 2008, 592).

3. $o(:) > œ(:) > e(:)$[12]

(4) ae. N. Sg. *dohter* (< germ. **dohtar* < idg. **dhughǝtér*[13])

  ae. D. Sg. *dehter*[14] 'Tochter'

  ae. N. Sg. *fōt* (< germ. **fōt(u)* < idg. **pōd–*) 'Fuß'

  ae. N. Pl. *fēt*[15] (< germ. **fōt–i–*) 'Füße'

  ae. N. Sg. *bōc* (< germ. **bōk–*) 'Buch'

  ae. N. Pl. *bēc* (< germ. **bōc–i–*) 'Bücher'

4. $u(:) > y(:)$

(5) ae. *gold* (< germ. **gulÞ–a*[16]) 'Gold'

---

12 Im Altenglischen werden die kurzen und langen mittleren gerundeten Vokale /o(:)/ durch *i*–Umlaut zunächst zu den vorderen gerundeten /œ(:)/, die sich dann wieder zu den entrundeten /e(:)/ verändern.

13 Idg. **dhughǝtér* wird durch den germ. *a*–Umlaut, in dem sich der hohe hintere Vokal /u/ vor /a, e, o/ in der Folgesilbe zu dem mittleren hinteren /o/ umwandelt, zu germ. **dohtar* entwickelt.

14 Für Dat. Sg. hat Idg. die Kasusendung **–ei*, die im Germ. als **–ī* erscheint. Germ. **dohtri* wird durch *i*–Umlaut zu ae. *dehter* und die Kasusendung germ. **–ī* geht im Altenglischen nach einer langen Stammsilbe verloren, die aus einem langen Vokal oder aus einem kurzen Vokal und einer folgenden Konsonantengruppe besteht (vgl. Bammesberger 1984b, 23).

15 Im Indogermanischen endet der Nom. Pl. in **–es*, das im Germ. zu **–iz* verändert wird. Diese Endung evoziert im Altenglischen *i*–Umlaut. **–z* ist nach der langen Stammsilbe geschwunden.

16 Durch den germ. *a*–Umlaut wird ae. *gold* aus germ. **gulÞ–a–* gebildet. D.h. das germanische /*u/ wird vor /a, e, o/ der Folgesilbe zu dem westgermanischen /o/ gesenkt.

ae. *gylden* (< germ. **guld–īna–*[17]) 'golden'

ae. *wull(o)* (< germ. **wullo*[18]) 'Wolle'

ae. *wyllen* 'wollen'

ae. *mūs* (< germ. **mūs–*) 'Maus'

ae. *mȳs* (< germ. **mūs–i–*) 'Mäuse'

5. *e* > *i*[19]

(6) ae. *birÞ* (< germ. **beriÞ(i)* < idg.**bher–e–ti–*[20]) 'er trägt'

Bei einigen Lehnwörtern im Altenglischen werden die Monophthonge /e(:)/ nicht nur durch *i*-Umlaut, sondern auch palatale Diphthongierung unter der Bedingung verändert, dass sie den palatalen Spiranten folgen (vgl. Baugh & Cable 1978, 77):

---

17 Mit Hilfe von dem Ableitungssuffix **–ina* wird das desubstantivische Adjektiv im Germ formuliert. Dieses Suffix induziert allerdings im Altenglischen *i*-Umlaut.

18 Der germanische *a*-Umlaut lässt sich bei germ. **wullo* nicht anwenden, weil dieser Prozess vor *l*-Gruppen unterbleibt (vgl. Pinsker 1974, 18).

19 Diese Veränderung kommt schon im Germ. zustanden. *Stricto sensu* muss daher /e/ > /i/ durch *i*-Umlaut aus der Erscheinung im Altenglischen ausgeschlossen zu werden. Trotzdem wird hier solche germanischer *i*-Umlaut auch als eine Kategorie behandelt, weil er sich im Ae. weiterhin ereignet.

20 Der thematische Vokal **–e–* im Idg. ist im Germ. zu **–i–* erhöht. Als der thematische Vokal wird derjenige benannt, welcher als ein Morphem für die Bildung eines Stamms mit Wurzel verbunden ist (vgl. Pei 1966, 272).

(7) lat. *cāseus* > **cǣsi* > **cēasi* > *cīese* 'Käse'

II. *i*-Umlaut der Diphthonge

1. *ea*[21] > *ie*[22]

(8) ae. *eald* (< wg. **alda*-) 'alt'

    ae. *ieldra* 'älter'   *ieldest*[23] 'ältest'

    ae. *healdan* 'halten'   *hielt* 'er hält'

2. *ēa*[24] > *īe*[25]

(9) germ. **hauz-ija*- > got. *hausjan*

              aws. *hīeran* 'hören'

             non-aws. *hēran*

---

21 Der Diphthong /ea/ im Altenglischen erweist sich als Ergebnis der sog. Brechung von kurzen /a/, die von J. Grimm(1967, Bd. 1, 82) terminologisiert worden ist und worunter die Diphthongierungen bestimmter kurzer Stammsilbevokale verstanden wird (vgl. Knobloch 1986, 386).

22 Im gesamten Gebiet des Altenglischen ist dieser Umlautprozess nicht zu finden, sondern kommt nur im Westsächsischen zum Vorschein. In anderen Dialektgebieten entwickelt sich /ea/ zu /e/ oder /æ/ (vgl. Brunner 1965, 77).

23 Neben der Superlativendung **-ōsta*- gibt es im Germ. auch **-ista*-, die *i*-Mutation verursacht.

24 Der Diphthong /ēa/ im Altenglischen entfaltet sich aus germ. /*au/.

25 Die durch *i*-Umlaut auftauchenden Diphthonge /i(:)e/ werden im Westsächsischen später zu /i(:)~y(:)/ entwickelt.

ae. *hēah* 'hoch'

ae. *hīehra* 'höher'   *hīehst* 'höchst'

3. *eo*[26] > *ie*

(10) ae. *heord* (< germ. **herdō*) 'Herde'

ae. *hierde* (< germ. **herd-ija-*) 'Hirt'

ae. *geong* 'jung'

ae. *giengra* 'jünger'   *giengst* 'jüngst'

4. *ēo*[27] > *ie*

(11) ae. *lēoht* (< germ. **leuhta-*) 'Licht'

ae. *līehtan* (< germ. **leuht-ija-*) 'leuchten'

ae. *cēosan* 'wahlen'

ae. *cīesÞ* 'er wählt'

2.2.2. Velarumlaut

Unter Velarumlaut (nach der englischen Terminologie Back Umlaut oder Mutation) sind im Allgemeinen diejenigen Veränderungen zu verstehen, bei denen die kurzen Monophthonge /a/ (oder /æ/), /e/, /i/ wegen des Einflusses

---

26 Der Diphthong /eo/ im Altenglischen erfindet sich als Ergebnis der Brechung von germanischem kurzem /e/.

27 Der Diphthong /ēo/ im Altenglischen entspricht dem germanischen /*eu/.

des folgenden vorhistorischen Hintervokals /u/ oder /o/ zu /ea/, /eo/, /io/ diphthongiert werden.[28] Im Englischen gehen diese phonologischen Erscheinungen in das 8. Jahrhundert, nämlich die uraltenglische Periode, zurück. Wie schon oben erwähnt, lässt sich der Velarumlaut je nach den umlautauslösenden Lauten wiederum in *u*-Umlaut und *o/a*-Umlaut subkategorisieren. Während bei dem ersten Fall das vorhistorische /u(:)/, wie auch dessen Ursprung immer aus dem germ. /u(:)/ oder /ō/ entstanden ist, als Faktor des Umlauts eindeutig wirkt, ist es dagegen bei dem letzteren unklar, ob das uraltenglische /o(:)/ oder dessen späteres historisches /a/ als mitwirkende Kraft fungiert. In Anschluss an K. Brunner(1965, 80) werden sie hier daher *u*-Umlaut und *o/a*-Umlaut genannt.[29] Wie der *i*-Umlaut zeigt sich der Velarumlaut im Altenglischen nicht einheitlich, sondern steht

---

[28] Neben dieser Diphthongierung kann dem Velarumlaut auch eine Art des kombinatorischen Lautwandels, der sog. gesteigerte Velarumlaut, zugerechnet werden, in denen die kurzen vorderen Vokale /i/, /e/ zu den kurzen hinteren /u/, /o/ werden, wenn ein Hintervokal /u/ oder /o/ in der Folgesilbe steht und außerdem der Halbvokal /w/ vorangeht. Dieser geht bei der englischen Sprachgeschichte früher vor sich als der diphthongierte Velarumlaut und etwa ins 7. Jh. datiert. Dabei geht es allerdings um die eigentümlichen mundartlichen Spezifika der ae. Schreibungen (vgl. Brunner 1965, 89–94; Hogg 1992, 115ff.; Lass/ Anderson 1975, 102–112; Luick 1921, 203ff.; Pinsker 1974, 25).

ags. *wicu* ~ ws. *wucu* (< germ. **wikōn*) 'Woche'
ws. *wita* ~ nh. *wuta* 'Weiser, Ratgeber'
ahd. *weralt*; nh. *woruld* ~ ws. *worold* 'Welt'
(< wg. **wira-aldō* < germ. **wera-* 'Mann, Mensch' + **aldra-* 'Alter')
ahd. *swester*; ws. *swostor* (< germ. **swester-*) 'Schwester'

[29] A. Campbell hat den Terminus *a*-Umlaut für allgemeiner gehalten, so dass er in seinem Buch 『Old English Grammar』(1959) *u*-Umlaut und *a*-Umlaut 'Back Umlaut' or 'Mutation' eingeordnet hat(vgl. Campbell 1974, 85).

und fällt mit den ae. Dialekten.

Der Velarumlaut darf nicht verwechselt werden mit der Brechung (engl. Breaking), die neben Verdumpfung und Aufhellung eine der von den übrigen wg. Dialekten auseinandergehaltenen anglofriesischen Besonderheiten aufweist und auf 2.–3. Jahrhundert zurückgeführt wird, obwohl der durch beide Phänomene wirkende Lautwandel einen „identical input and structural change" (Jones 1980, 126) hat. Denn die Bedingungen des Vorkommens von Velarumlaut und Brechung sind von ganz verschiedener Art. Bei der Brechung wird ein Gleitvokal vor den folgenden bestimmten Konsonantengruppen epenthetisch eingeschoben, bei dem Velarumlaut dagegen vor dem Hintervokal der Folgesilbe. Darüber hinaus betrifft Brechung nur kurze Vokale. Zur Kennzeichnung der altenglischen Brechung ist es also hilfreich, sie kontrastiv mit den zu dem Westgermanischen gehörigen Sprachvarietäten, hier mit dem Althochdeutschen, zu vergleichen:

(12) Brechung

    ae. *eahta*; ahd. *ahto* 'acht' (< wg. **ahto* < germ. **ahtau*)

    ae. *eorÞe*; ahd. *erda* 'Erde' (< germ. **erÞō*)

    ae. *miox* ~ *meox*; ahd. *mist* 'Mist' (< germ. **mihstu–*)

I. *u*-Umlaut

1. *a > ea*

(13) ae. *heafuc* ~ hafoc; ahd. *habuh* 'Habicht' (< germ. **habuka–*)

ae. *featu*[30] ~ *fatu* 'Fässer'

(Sg. ae. *fæt*; ahd. *faz* 'Fass' < germ. **fata-*)

ae. *fearu* ~ *fare* 'ich fahre'

(Inf. ae. *faran*; ahd. *faran* < germ. **far-a-*)

2. *e* > *eo*

(14) ae. *teoru*[31] 'Teer' (< germ. **terwja-/jōn*)

ae. *eofor* ~ *efor*; ahd. *ebur* 'Eber' (< wg. **ebura-*)

ae. *meodu* ~ *medu*; ahd. *metu* ~ *meto* ~ *met* 'Met'

(< germ. **medu-*)

3. *i* > *io*

(15) ae. *mioluc* ~ *meoluc*; ahd. *miluh* ~ *milih* 'Milch'

(< germ. **meluk-*)

ae. *liomu* ~ *leomu* 'Glieder'

(Sg. ae. *lim*; ahd. *gilid* 'Glied' < germ. **liÞu-*)

ae. *sioluc* ~ *sīde*; ahd. *sīda*[32] 'Seide'

---

30 Um einen Pl. zu bilden wird im Altenglischen die Endung /u/ dem zu der Klasse des germanischen *a*-Stamms (und des indogermanischen *o*-Stamms) gehörigen neutralen Substantiv hinzufügt. Diese Endung ruft gegebenfalls auch Verlarumlaut hervor.

31 Das entsprechende deutsche Wort wird seit dem 16. Jahrhundert in hochdeutschen Texten bezeugt(vgl. Kluge 1989, 725).

32 Das Wort ist entlehnt aus dem mittellateinischen *seta*, wahrscheinlich über eine

II. *o/a*-Umlaut

1. *a > ea*

(16) ae. *fearaÞ* ~ *faraÞ* 'wir fahren'

  (Inf. ae. *faran*; ahd. *faran* < germ. **far-a-*)

  ae. Gen. Dat. Sg. *ealoÞ* ~ *aloÞ* (Nom. *ealu* 'Bier')

  ae. *heafoc* ~ *hafoc*; ahd. *habuh* 'Habicht' (< germ. **habuka-*)

2. *e > eo*

(17) ae. *heolan* ~ *helan*; ahd. *helan* 'hehlen' (< germ. **hel-a-*)

  ae. *eotan* ~ *etan*; ahd. *azzan* 'essen' (< germ. **et-a-*)

  ae. *spreocan* ~ *sprecan*; ahd. *sp(r)ehhan* 'sprechen'

  (< wg. **sprek-a-*)

3. *i > io*

(18) ae. *liofaÞ* ~ *lifaÞ* 'er lebt'

  (Inf. ae. *libban* ~ *lifian* ~ *leofian*; ahd. *lebēn* < germ. **lib-ǣ-*)

  ae. *nioman* ~ *niman*; ahd. *neman* 'nehmen' (< germ. **nem-a-*)

  ae. *nioÞor* ~ *niÞer*; ahd. *nidar* 'nieder' (< germ. **niÞra-*)

---

romanische Sprache (vgl. Kluge 1989, 664).

3. Funktionen des *i*-Umlats

Sprachhistorisch gesehen war der Umlaut ursprünglich eine rein phonetisch bedingte Vokalalternation mit Assimilationscharakter, noch genauer ein kontextabhängiges Allophon. Durch den Schwund bzw. nach der Neutralisierung der umlautbewirkenden Segmente /i/, /ī/ und /j/ in unbetonten Silben ging aber der Prozess der Phonemisierung der ursprünglichen Umlaut-Allophone vor sich. Dies besagt, dass Alternationen, die historisch gesehen auf dem Umlaut beruhen, nicht mehr abhängig von den phonetischen Eigenschaften der Folgesilbe waren und dass eine Umlautvariante im Laufe der Sprachentwicklung wie ihr entsprechendes nicht umgelautetes Phonem phonologisiert wurden.

Weiter ist in Betracht zu ziehen, dass die phonemisierten Umlautvokale innerhalb der verschiedenen grammatischen Kategorien der Flexion und der Wortbildung morphologische Relevanz bekamen. D.h. der Umlaut war mit einer bestimmten grammatischen Funktion zusammengefallen. In diesem Zusammenhang kann man von der Morphologisierung des Umlauts sprechen.

Hinsichtlich der Funktionen des *i*-Umlauts werden hier nur phonologische und morphologische Ebene jeweilig zur Sprache gebracht.

3.1. Phonologische Ebene

Diachron gesehen hat der *i*-Umlaut die phonologische Ebene einer Sprache dadurch verändert, dass er zunächst als Allophon bestanden und später als ein eigenes Phonem, also als bedeutungsunterscheidende Einheit, im Sprachsystem eine feste Stelle eingenommen hat. Vor der Behandlung des einzelnen Einflusses des *i*-Umlauts auf das phonologische System einer Sprache ist es nützlich, die Typologie des historischen Phonemwandels zu erwähnen. Dadurch kann man den *i*-Umlaut im Hinblick auf die diachronische Phonologie noch besser verstehen.

Das Phonemsystem einer Sprache kann nicht nur durch endogene Sprachveränderungen, also die inneren Veränderungen einer betreffenden Sprache bzw. Spachvariante, beeinflusst werden, sondern auch in Bezug auf exogene Sprachänderungen, in denen nach dem Vorbild einer anderen Sprache bzw. Sprachvariante eine Reihe von neuen Phonemen entlehnt wird oder die vorhandene Phonemdistribution anderes zur Durchführung kommt (vgl. Szulc 1987, 17). Der *i*-Umlaut betrifft also die endogenen Sprachveränderungen, weil er innerhalb einer betreffenden Sprache bzw. Variante ohne Einfluss einer anderen die Umgestaltung des Phonemsystems ins Rollen bringt.

Bezüglich der endogenen Sprachveränderungen sind die Typen des Phonemwandels (vgl. Görlach 1982, 48ff.; Penzl 1971, 23ff.; Szulc 1987, 10-16; Weimann 1982, 69f.) einzuteilen in:

(1) Phonemverschiebung (Umphonologisierung),

(2) Phonemspaltung (Phonologisierung, Divergenz),

(3) Phonemzusammenfall,

(4) Phonemschwund,

(5) Biphonematisierung (Diphonemisierung, Fission),

(6) Fusion (Monophonematisierung),

(7) Epenthesierung,

(8) Metathese,

(9) morphologisch bedingter Phonemwandel usw.

Davon bilden Phonemspaltung, Phonemzusammenfall und morphologisch bedingter Phonemwandel einen Zusammenhang mit dem *i*-Umlaut. Daher werden in diesem Aufsatz nur diese drei Phonemwandeltypen betrachtet.

3.1.1. *i*-Umlaut als eine bei der Phonemspaltung mitwirkende Kraft

Die ursprünglich stellungsbedingten Allophone eines Phonems können sich zu verschiedenen selbständigen Phonemen verändern, indem sie nicht mehr in phonetisch komplementärer Distribution stehen. Die allophonische Opposition entwickelt sich also zu der phonemischen Opposition (vgl. Moulton 1967, 1394). Dabei ist von Phonemspaltung die Rede. Mittels dieses Prozesses vergrößert sich das Phoneminventar einer gegebenen Sprache.

(19) urae. **mūs*, **mūsi* > urae. **mūs*, **mȳsi* > ae. *mūs*, *mȳs* 'Maus, Mäuse'

Im Uraltenglischen stehen zwei Allophone [ū~ȳ] eines Phonems /ū/ in der komplementären Distribution wie Ich-Laut [ç] und Ach-Laut [x] im Deutschen, in der sie nie in gleicher Umgebung vorkommen, im Vorgang der Sprachentwicklung bilden beide jedoch ein Minimalpaar und treten in Opposition auf. Sie werden damit also jeweilig zu den eigenen Phonemen.

3.1.2. *i*-Umlaut als Phonemzusammenfall

Der Phonemzusammenfall kann wieder in den vollständigen und den unvollständigen unterteilt werden. Bei dem ersten sind zwei oder mehrere oppositionsbildende Phoneme lediglich zu einer distinktiven Einheit verschmolzen und bei dem letzteren bildet dagegen ein Allophon eines Phonems zusammen mit einem Allophon eines anderen Phonems eine neue Einheit (vgl. Görlach 1982, 49; Szulc 1987, 12f.; Weimann 1982, 70). Diesen betrifft eine durch *i*-Umlaut hervorgerufene Erscheinung.

(20) ahd. N. Sg. *lamb* 'Lamm'   ahd. N. Pl. *lẹmbir* 'Lämmer'

ahd. *nëman* 'nehmen'

(21) ae. N. Sg. *gōs* 'Gans'   ae. N. Pl. *gēs* 'Gänse'

ae. *bēte* 'Rübe'

Im Althochdeutschen fallen das durch den sog. Primärumlaut erzeugte kurze geschlossene /e/<ẹ>, das von einem Allophon des germanischen kurzen /a/ ausgegangen ist, mit dem ursprünglichen kurzen offenen /e/<ë>, das dem urgerm. /*e/ entspricht, zusammen. Das /e/ im Althochdeutschen besitzt also zwei Allophone [e~ɛ], die im Lauf der Sprachentwicklung zu /e/<ẹ> und /ɛ/<ë> werden (vgl. Braune 1953, 27), wobei es sich um eine Phonomspaltung handelt. Solche Phonemzusammenfall gilt auch für /œ(:)/, das durch den *i*-Umlaut aus /o(:)/ entstanden ist, und /e(:)/ im Altenglischen.

3.1.3. *i*-Umlaut als morphologisch bedingte Phonemwandel

Morphe, die dieselbe Bedeutung haben und deren unterschiedliche sprachliche Formen nicht phonologisch bedingt sind, formulieren nur dann eine Reihe von Allomorphen eines Morphems, insofern sie voneinander in komplementärer Beziehung stehen. Solche Allomorphe werden morphologisch determiniert genannt (vgl. Bühler et al. 1983, 81). Unter dem morphologisch bedingten Phonemwandel versteht man also, dass ein Phonem kraft Analogie für das Kennzeichen eines Morphmes von einem anderen Phonem substituiert wird (vgl. Szulc 1987, 16). Vorzugsweise tritt morphologisch bedingter Phonemwandel bei Lehnwörtern häufig ein.

(22) mhd. Sg. *walt*   mhd. Pl. *wälde* 'Wälder'

    mhd. Sg. *general*   mhd. Pl. *generäle* ~ *generale*

                          'Generäle ~ Generale'

Das Wort *general* wird in der mhd. Zeit aus dem Lateinischen entlehnt. Sein Plural hat jedoch durch morphologische Analogie unabhängig von der phonologischen Bedingung ein umgelautetes Phonem in seinem Stamm.

3.2. Morphologische Ebene

Im Allgemeinen ist man sich darüber einig, dass der anfangs phonologisch bedingte Wandel in der Sprachentwicklung die morphologischen Funktionen einnehmen kann (vgl. Robinson 1975, 1). Dazu gehören in erster Linie Ablaut,

Vernersches Gesetz bzw. grammatischer Wechsel und Umlaut. Der *i*-Umlaut hat einen bedeutsamen Einfluss auf den morphologischen Bereich sowohl im Altenglischen wie in den gesamten Stufen des Deutschen (vgl. Bammesberger 1989, 71; Benett 1969, 18; Wurzel 1984, 663), obwohl sich im heutigen Englischen *i*-Umlaut als irregular, unproduktiv und vereinzelt erweist.

Die Entwicklung des *i*-Umlauts auf die morphologische Sphäre wird hier je nach der einzelnen Wortklasse dargelegt.

3.2.1. *i*-Umlaut im Substantiv

Für die Markierung des Kasusmorphems und/oder des Pluralmorphems kann der Umlaut mit anderen zusätzlichen Ausdrucksmitteln oder ohne sie im Altenglischen und in den gesamten Perioden des Deutschen benutzt werden.

(23) ae. N. Sg. *man* D. Sg. *men* N./A. Pl. *men* 'Männer'

ae. N. Sg. *burg* G./D. Sg. *byrig* N./A. Pl. *byrig* 'Burgen'

nhd. Sg. *Vater* Pl. *Väter*

nhd. Sg. *Dorf* Pl. *Döfer*

3.2.1.1. Wurzelnomina[33] im Altenglischen

Der *i*-Umlaut im Dat. Sg. und Nom./Akk. Pl.[34] der Wurzelnomina beruht

---

[33] Wurzelnomina sind ein fundamentaler Typus der konsonantischen Deklinationsklasse, in der sich die Kasusendungen und die Numerusendungen direkt an die auf Konsonanten endenden Stämme anschließen.

auf der Endung des Dat. Sg. *-i- und der Endung des Nom. Pl. *-iz. Im Unterschied zu Maskulina haben die Feminina dieser Gruppe auch i-Umlaut im Gen. Sg., der sich aus der germanischen Endung *-iz (< idg. *-is) erklärt:

(24) ae. N. Sg. (m) fōt   D. Sg. fēt 'Fuß'   N./A. Pl. fēt 'Füße'

 ae. N. Sg. (f) bōc   D. Sg. bēc 'Buch'   G. Sg. bēc 'Buches'

 N./A. Pl. bēc 'Bücher'

Im Zusammenhang mit dem Verschwinden der Kasusendungen im Mittelenglischen, Synkretismus,[35] besitzen die wenigen Wörter dieser Klasse die Form ohne Umlaut im Sg. und die Form mit Umlaut im Pl., während die anderen im Pl. selbst den Umlaut verlieren(vgl. Bammesberger 1989, 92; Schirmunski 1961, 144):

(25) ne. foot – feet   goose – geese   man – men

 ne. book – books   oak – oaks   night – nights

3.2.1.2. Substantive mit -r-Stämme[36]

Der i-Umlaut in den Substantiven dieser Gruppe erscheint im Gegensatz

---

34 Der Akk. Pl. im Altenglischen ist eigentlich dem Nom. Pl. nachgebildet.

35 Als Synkretismus wird formaler Zusammenfall verschiedener grammatischer Funktion, insbesondere im Kasussystem, bezeichnet (vgl. Bußmann 2008, 708).

36 Die Substantive mit Stämme auf idg. *-er/-or bezeichnen die Verwandtschaft.

zu Wurzelnomina nur im Dat. Sg.

(26) ae. N./ G./ A. Sg. *dohtor*   D. Sg. *dehter* 'der Tochter'

   N./ A. Pl. *dohtor* 'Töchter'

 ae. N./ G./ A. Sg. *brōÞor*   D. Sg. *brēÞer* 'dem Bruder'

   N./ A. Pl. *brōÞor* 'Brüder'

Die Gründe dafür sind folgend(vgl. Brunner 1965, 229):

1. Abfallen des *-i-* in der Pluralendung *-iz* vor *-z* nach unbetonten Silben, bevor der Umlaut eintritt;

2. Augehen des Gen. Sg. von der idg. Endung *-os*.

3.2.1.3. Substantive mit *-nd*-Stämme[37]

Bei den Substantiven auf *-nd* werden die Formen im Dat. Sg. und Nom./ Akk. Pl. durch den *i*-Umlaut beeinflusst.

(27) ae. N. A. Sg. *frēond*[38]   D. Sg. *frīend* 'dem Freund'

   N./ A. Pl. *frīend* 'Freunde'

Die Ursache dieses Umlautprozesses ist gleich der bei Wurzelnomina.

---

37 Diese Klasse wird von den substantivierten *Partizipia präsentis* geformt.

38 Ae. *frēond* geht von der Partizipialbildung zu germ. **frijôjan* 'lieben' aus(vgl. OED 1989, Bd. 6, 192).

3.2.2. *i*-Umlaut im Adjektiv

Im Altenglischen und Deutschen kann eine Gruppe von Adjektiven mit Hilfe von *i*-Umlaut und bestimmten Endungen das Komparativmorphem und das Superlativmorphem in Worte kleiden. In der Sprachentwicklung hat die durch *i*-Umlaut bildende Komparation im Deutschen nach wie vor die große Produktivität, während im Englischen die Tendenz zur Bildung ohne Umlaut vorherrscht, wenn auch nur wenige Wörter für den Ausdruck der Steigerungsstufen umgelautet werden.

Das Germanische hat zwei Endungen *-izan-*, *-ozan-* für den Komparativ und *-ista-*, *-osta-* für den Superlativ. Die Bindevokale *-i-*, *-o-* in der Form des Komparativs sind in der Entwicklung zum Ae. durch Synkope[39] ausgefallen, was die Vermischung beider Typen begünstigte. Dagegen werden sie im Superlativ zu *-e-* (< *-i-*) oder *-o-* (< *-o-*) verändert (vgl. Schirmunski 1961, 146). Allerdings fungiert *-i-* in *-izan-*, *-ista-* als Faktor des Umlauts:

[1] ohne Umlaut

(28) ae. *earm* (< germ. *arma-*) 'arm'

---

39 Als ein Typus der Kontraktion wird unter Synkope die Elision eines unbetonten Vokals innerhalb eines Wortes verstanden. Daneben können als Kontraktion erwähnt werden:
   1. Aphärese, d.h. Wegfall anlautender sprachlicher Elemente, z.B. ne. *amid ~ mid*; nhd. *heraus ~ raus*;
   2. Apokope, d.h. Auslassung eines oder mehrerer Sprachlaute am Wortende, z.B. germ. *mūsiz* > ae. *mȳs*; nhd. *dem Tage ~ dem Tag*.

earmra (< germ. **arm‒o‒zan‒*) 'ärmer'

earmost (< germ. **arm‒o‒sta‒*) 'ärmst'

ae. *heard ‒ heardra ‒ heardost* 'hart ‒ härter ‒ härtest'

[2] mit Umlaut

(29) ae. *eald* (< germ. **alda‒*) 'alt'

ieldra (< germ. **ald‒i‒zan*) 'älter'

ieldest (< germ. **ald‒i‒sta*) 'ältest'

ae. *lang ‒ lengra ‒ lengest* 'lang ‒ länger ‒ längst'

ae. *strang ‒ strengra ‒ strengest* 'stark ‒ stärker ‒ stärkst'

Da im Englischen die Neigung zur Komparationsbildung ohne Umlaut vorwiegt, zeigt sich im Neuenglischen nur eine Form mit Umlaut wie *elder*, *eldest* neben *older*, *oldest* in verschiedenen Bedeutungen:

(30) *Tom is older than Betty.* 'Tom ist älter als Betty.'

Tom is his elder brother. 'Tom ist sein älterer Bruder.'

3.2.3. *i*-Umlaut im Verb

Im Altenglischen ‒ wenn auch in den Dialekten verschieden ‒ und im Deutschen ist der Umlaut in den 2. und 3. Person Präsens Indikativ der starken Verben zu finden, wenn der Stammvokal ihn zulässt. Diesen Vorgang führt die germanischen Endungen **-is(t)* und **-iÞ* für die

Morpheme {2. und 3. Person, Präsens, Indikativ} herbei:

(31) nhd. *ich fahre – du fährst* (ahd. feris), *er fährt* (ahd. ferit)

ae. *ic bere – Þū bir(e)st ~ bires, hē bir(e)Þ* 'tragen'

Für das Kennzeichen der 2. und 3. Person Präsens Indikativ kommen im Altenglischen zwei Typen der Formen vor (vgl. Brunner 1965, 285; Moore/ Knott 1977, 181; Schirmunski 1961, 146):

1. Formen mit synkopierter Endung, d.h. Kontraktion des Bindevokals *–e–* (< germ. *–i–), und Umlaut in der Stammsilbe in den südlichen westsächsischen Texten;

2. Formen mit bewahrten unbetonten *–e–* und umlautloser Stammsilbe in den weiteren mundartlichen Gebieten:

(32) ae. *ic fealle, Þū fiels(t) ~ fealles, hē fielÞ ~ fealleÞ* 'fallen'

ae. *ic lūce, Þū lȳcs(t) ~ lūces, hē lȳcÞ ~ lūceÞ* 'schließen'

Diese zwei Typen finden sich auch bei der durch den germanischen *i*-Umlaut induzierten Veränderung *e > i*:

(33) urgerm. *beriÞ > germ. *biriÞ > ws. *bireÞ* 'er trägt'

urgerm. *helpis > germ. *hilpis > ws. *hilps* 'du hilfst'

Der formale Unterschied zwischen altenglischen Dialekten ist schon im

Spätaltenglischen durch die Formen ohne Umlaut ausgeglichen. Dieser Zusammenhang basiert wahrscheinlich darauf, dass der Umlaut kein einziges Markierungmittel für die Morpheme {2. und 3. Person, Präsens, Indikativ}, sondern nur ein zusätzliches Kennzeichen neben der Personalendung ist (vgl. Brunner 1965, 285f.; Schirmunski 1961, 147). Der durch Analogie auftretende Ausgleichungsprozess ist im Englischen sehr häufig.

4. Schlussbemerkung

Fassen wir noch einmal kurz zusammen: Der Umlaut, unter dem der Qualitätswechsel eines betonten Vokals durch den unbetonten Vokal der Folgesilbe verstanden wird, war, historisch gesehen, eine rein phonetische stellungsbedingte Erscheinung. Der Schwund bzw. der Veränderung der umlautverursachenden Faktoren führte jedoch nur dann zur Entwicklung von Umlautsallophonen zu Umlautsphonemen, wenn die Allophone auch in der neuen phonetischen Umgebung ihre alte Umlautsqualität bewahrten. Dieser Umlautwechsel erzielte in einer einzelsprachlichen Entwicklung bestimmte morphologische Leistungen.

Ich will mich an dieser Stelle nur mit der folgenden Anmerkung begnügen: In der Entwicklung des Englischen können im Allgemeinen drei große Entwicklungsstufen angenommen werden. Das Altenglische, in dem viele Wortarten nach Kasus, Person, Numerus, Genus, Tempus, Modus usw. flektiert werden, fügte sich in das Mittelenglische, die Ära der ausgeglichenen

Flexion. Aufgrund des Gesetzes der Analogie wird sowohl auf die Deklination als auch die Konjugation im Neuenglischen letztlich verzichtet. Damit hängt die normale Sprachentwiclung von synthetischer zu analytischer Struktur eng zusammen. Diese Neigung macht auch bei dem *i*-Umlaut keine Ausnahme. Im Altenglischen wurde der *i*-Umlaut relativ häufig verwendet und im Mittelenglischen war die Ausgleichungsform, d.h. die Form ohne den *i*-Umlaut, vorherrschend. Im heutigen Englischen werden die Alternationen, die diachronisch gesehen auf der Umlauterscheinung basieren, unregelmäßig, okkasionell und verstreut auftreten, weil sie keine morphologische und grammatische Produktivität mehr besitzen.

Wie oben schon nachdrücklich behauptet, ist für die Forschung der Sprachgeschichte keine Isolierung bzw. Zusammenhanglosigkeit zwischen Synchronie und Diachronie, sondern Kooperation bzw. Zusammenwirken beider Betrachtungsweisen notwendig. Ohne diese Harmonie können wir die Entwicklung unserer Sprache nicht richtig verstehen, weil zu keiner Zeit die Sprache zum Stillstand kommt, d.h. sie sich hic et nunc ohne Unterbrechung entwickelt und ihr 'Aussehen' andauernd umgestaltet.

Abkürzungen

ae.	altenglisch	lat.	lateinisch
afrz.	altfranzösisch	mhd.	mittelhochdeutsch
ags.	angelsächsisch	ne.	neuenglisch
ahd.	althochdeutsch	nh.	nordholländisch
aisl.	altisländisch	nhd.	neuhochdeutsch
Akk.	Akkusativ	Nom.	Nominativ
aws.	altwestsächisch	Pl.	Plural
Dat.	Dativ	Sg.	Singular
Gen.	Genitiv	urae.	uraltenglisch
germ.	germanisch	urgerm.	urgermanisch
got.	gotisch	vlat.	vulgärlateinisch
idg.	indogermanisch	wg.	westgermanisch
Inf.	Infinitiv	ws.	westsächisch
KHM	Kim Hyeong Min		

Symbolverzeichnisse

<...>	Spitze Klammern für orthographische Wiedergabe
[...]	Eckige Klammern für phonetische Transkription
/.../	Schrägestriche für phonologische Transkription
{...}	Geschweifte Klammern für Morpheme
>	Rechtsgerichtete spitze Klammer für »wird zu«
/	Alternative Ausdrücke
*	Asterisk für ungrammatische/nicht akzeptable Ausdrücke

Literatur

Allgemeine Sprachwissenschaft (1973), Bd. 1: Existenzformen, Funktionen und Geschichte der Sprache, Von einem Autorenkollektiv unter der Leitung von B. A. Serébrennikow, Ins Deutsche übertragen und herausgegeben von Hans Zikmund und Günter Feudel, München & Salzburg.

Bammesberger, Alfred (1984a), English Etymology, Heidelberg.

Bammesberger, Alfred (1984b), A Sketch of Diachronic English Morphology, Regenburg. (= Schriftenreihe der Katholischen Universität Eichstätt; 7: Abteilung Sprache und Literatur)

Bammesberger, Alfred (1989), English Linguistics, Heidelberg.

Bennett, Hobart (1969), "Manifestations of *i*-Umlaut in Old English," *Linguistics* 50, 5–26.

Braune, Wilhelm (1953), *Althochdeutsche Grammatik*, Bearbeitet von Walther Mitzka, 8. Auflage, Tübingen.

Brunner, Karl (1965), *Altenglische Grammatik*, Nach der angelsächsischen Grammatik von Eduard Sievers, 3., neubearbeitete Auflage, Tübingen.

Bühler, Hans *et al*. (1983), *Linguistik I. Lehr- und Übungsbuch zur Einführung in die Sprachwissenschaft*, 5., unveränderte Auflage, Tübingen.

Bußmann, Hadumod (2008), *Lexikon der Sprachwissenschaft*, 4., durchgesehene und bibliographisch ergänzte Auflage unter Mitarbeit von Hartmut Lauffer, Mit 34 Graphiken, 14 Tabellen und 8 Abbildungen, Stuttgart.

Campbell, A. (1974), *Old English Grammar* (1959[1]), 6. Edition, Oxford.

Coseriu, Eugenio (1975), "Synchronie, Diachronie und Typologie," Cherubim, Dieter (Hrsg.), *Sprachwandel. Reader zur diachronischen Sprachwissenschaft*, Berlin & New York, 134–149.

Faiß, Klaus (1989), *Englische Sprachgeschichte*, Tübingen.

Görlach, Manfred (1982), *Einführung in die englischen Sprachgeschichte*, 2., überarbeitete Auflage, Heidelberg.

Grimm, Jacob (1967), *Deutsche Grammatik*(1822[1]), Hrsg. von Wilhelm Scherer, Nachdruck der Ausgabe Berlin 1870, Hildesheim.

Hogg, Richard M. (1992), "Phonology and Morphology,". Hogg, Richard M. (Ed.), The Cambridge History of the English Language, Vol. The Beginnings to 1066, Cambridge.

Jones, Charles (1980), "Rounding and Fronting in Old English Phonology: A Dependency Approach," *Folia Linguistica Historica* 1, 125‒137.

Kim, Hyeong Min (2004), "Diagnostische Kriterien der Markiertheitsbestimmung," 독일언어문학 25, 31‒57.

Kim, Hyeong Min (2006), "Der Einfluss des *i*-Umlauts auf die Wortbildung. Vor allem unter Berücksichtigung des Altenglischen, 서강인문논총 20, 161‒188.

Knobloch, Johann (1986), *Sprachwissenschaftliches Wörterbuch*, Bd. I, Heidelberg.

Kranzmayer, Eberhard (1956), *Historische Lautgeographie des gesamtbairischen Dialektraumes*, Wien.

Kluge, Friedrich (1989), *Etymologisches Wörterbuch der deutschen Sprache*, Unter Mithilfe von Max Bürgisser und Bernd Grego völlig neu bearbeitet von Elmar Seebold, 22. Auflage, Berlin & New York.

Lass, Roger & Anderson, John M. (1975), *Old English Phonology*, Cambridge.

Lewandowski, Theodor (1990), *Linguistische Wörterbuch*, 5., überarbeitete Auflage, Heidelberg & Wiesbaden.

Linke, Angelika & Nussbaumer, Markus & Portmann, Paul R. (1996), *Studienbuch Linguistik*, Ergänzt um ein Kapitel »Phonetik und Phonologie« von Urs Willi, 3., unveränderte Auflage, Tübingen. (= Reihe Germanistische Lingistik; 121: Kollegbuch)

Luick, Karl (1921), *Historische Grammatik der englischen Sprache* (1914[1]), Leipzig.

Moore, Samuel & Knott, Thomas A. (1977), *The Elements of Old English. Elementary Grammar Reference Grammar and Reading Selections* (1955[1]), Ann Arbor & Michigan.

Moulton, William G. (1967), "Types of Phonemic Change," *To Honor Roman Jakobson. Essays on the Occasion of his Seventieth Birthday, 11. October 1966*, Vol. II, The Hague & Paris, 1393‒1407.

Pei, Mario (1966), *Glossary of Linguistic Terminology*, New York & London.

Penzl, Herbert (1971), *Lautsystem und Lautwandel in den althochdeutschen Dialekten*, München.

Pinsker, Hans Ernst (1974), *Historische englische Grammatik. Elemente der Laut-, Formen- und Wortbildungslehre* (1959[1]), 4. Auflage, München.

Robinson, Orrin W. (1975), "Abstract Phonology and the History of Umlaut," *Lingua* 37, 1-29.

Scheuringer, Hermann (1992), "Die grammatikalische Erklärung von Sprachvariation," *Zeitschrift für Phonetik, Sprachwissenschaft und Kommunikationsforschung* 45, 481-494.

Schirmunski, Viktor (1961), "Der Umlaut im Englischen und Deutschen. Ein historisch-grammatischer Vergleich," *Zeitschrift für Anglistik und Amerikanistik 9*, 139-153.

Schweikle, Günther (1987), *Germanisch-deutsche Sprachgeschichte im Überblick*, 2., verbesserte und ergänzte Auflage, Stuttgart.

Seidelmann, Erich (1987), "Über die Arten von Lautveränderungen,". Gabriel, Eugen & Stricker, Hans (Hrsg.), *Probleme der Dialektgeographie*, 8. Arbeitstagung alemannischer Dialektologen Triesenberg, Fürstentum Liechtenstein, 20.-22. September 1984, Bühl & Baden, 200-214.

Szulc, Aleksander (1987), *Historische Phonologie des Deutschen*, Tübingen. (= Sprachstrukturen: Reihe A, Historische Sprachstrukturen; 6)

Weimann, Klaus (1982), *Einführung ins Altenglische*, Heidelberg.

Wurzel, Wolfgang (1984), Was bezeichnet der Umlaut im Deutschen? *Zeitschrift für Phonetik, Sprachwissenschaft und Kommunikationsforschung* 37, 647-663.

언어별 음절 연구와 국어 음절의 특징

신승용

1. 서론

음절은 음운 현상이 일어나는 핵심적인 단위이다. 생성음운론 이전에 음절은 주로 음성학적인 관점에서 다루어졌다. 그리고 Chomsky and Halle (1968)의 초기 생성 음운론에서도 음절은 음운론적인 관점에서 다루어지지 않았는데, 그것은 음절을 도입하지 않아도 음소배열제약으로 충분히 설명할 수 있다고 보았기 때문이다.

음운 현상의 기술에 음운론적 단위로써 음절을 도입해야 함을 적극적으로 제기한 것은 Hooper(1972)에서이다. 그리고 음절을 음운 층위와 독립된 자립분절 단위로 음운론적 기술에 도입한 것은 Khan(1976)에서라고 할 수 있다. 이러한 흐름의 연장선에서 Selkirk(1982:337)은 음소배열제약을 가장 일반적이고 가장 설명적으로 타당하게 설명하기 위해서, 그리고 음운 규칙의 적용 범위의 성격을 설명하기 위해서, 또한 강세나 성조 등의 초분절적인 음운 현상을 설명하기 위해서 음절이 음운론적으로 필요한 단위라고 주장하였다. Khan(1976)의 음절은 음절이 분절음과 직접 연결되는 구조였는데,

Clement and Keyser(1983)는 음절과 분절음 사이에 골격 층렬(skeletal-tier)이 있는 음절구조를 제안하면서, 본격적으로 음절 음운론이 출발하게 되었다.

음운론적 교체가 실질적으로 일어나는 단위는 형태소나 단어가 아니라 음절이다. 즉 음절 경계에서 또는 음절 내부에서 교체가 일어난다. 그런데 음절구조나 음절의 특성이 언어마다 다르기 때문에, 이러한 구조적인 차이가 교체의 내용이나 양상에도 차이를 유발한다. 그런 점에서 음절과 관련된 차이를 살펴보는 것은 각 언어의 특징을 파악하는 데에도 유용하다. 또한 국어의 자음과 관련된 통합관계에의 음운 현상은 대부분은 음절말과 음절초 자음의 관계에서 일어난다. 그렇기 때문에 음절 및 음절구조에 대한 이해는 음운 현상의 본질을 밝히는 데에도 중요하다. 이러한 관점에서 본고에서는 음절구조, 골격 층렬의 음운론적 성격, 활음의 음절구조상에서의 위치에 대해 언어학적인 관점에서 그리고, 국어학적인 관점에서 살펴보고자 한다.

2장에서는 음절구조에 대한 언어학적인 논의를 정리하면서, 다른 언어의 음절구조의 특성과의 비교를 통해서 국어의 음절구조를 밝힐 것이다. 그리고 3장에서는 음절과 분절음 사이에 존재한다고 가정되는 골격 층렬의 음운론적 성격에 대해 살펴볼 것이다. 음운론적으로 골격 층렬이 음운론적 단위로 실재한다고 보아야 하는 언어가 있는데, 국어도 과연 음운론적 실재로서 존재한다고 볼 수 있는지를 규명할 것이다. 마지막으로 4장에서는 모음에 선행하는 활음이 음절초 요소인지 음절핵 요소인지에 대해 논의할 것이다. 언어마다 모음에 선행하는 활음이 음절초에 연결되는지, 음절핵에 연결되는지는 차이가 있다. 다른 언어에서 모음에 선행하는 활음의 특성을 살펴보면서, 국어에서 모음에 선행하는 활음이 음절초에 연결되는지, 음절핵에 연결되는지를 규명할 것이다.

2. 음절구조의 유형과 국어의 음절구조

음절 음운론이 이론적으로 정립되면서 언어별로 음절구조가 어떠한지에 대한 논의가 활발하게 일어났다. 이론적으로 상정 가능한 음절구조가 어차 피 몇 개 되지 않는다. 그래서 음절구조에 대한 논의를 단순화하면 결국 (1ㄱ-ㄷ) 중에 어떤 구조이냐에 대한 것으로 정리된다. 물론 Levin(1985)에 서 제안한 N의 최대투사로서의 음절구조도 있고,[1] 모라 음운론에서 제안한 모라 구조도 있다. 그렇지만 음절 음운론에서 음절구조를 논할 때는 일반적 으로 (1ㄱ-ㄷ) 중의 어떤 구조이냐에 대한 것이다. 일반적으로 (1ㄱ)을 삼지 적 구조, (1ㄴ)을 우분지 구조, (1ㄷ)을 좌분지 구조라고 통칭한다.

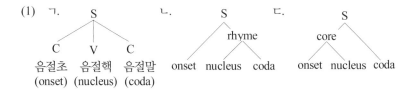

Fuge(1987:360)는 (1ㄴ)의 우분지 구조가 분포 제약이나 발화 실수, 단어 게임 등을 통해서 볼 때 가장 보편적인 음절구조라고 하였다. 그리고 (1ㄷ) 의 좌분지 구조는 논리적으로는 가능하지만 세계의 어느 언어도 이 구조를 가졌다고 보고된 바 없다고 말하기도 하였다. 그런데 국어의 음절구조를 다룬 논의들 중에는 Fuge(1987)가 논리적으로 가능하지만 실제 존재하지 않

---

1 N(음절핵)이 음절말과 결합하여 N'를 이루고, 이 N'가 음절초와 결합하여 N''를 형성한 다. 그래서 음절을 N의 최대투사라고 한다. 이는 X'-이론, 즉 XP를 X의 최대투사로 보 는 생성문법의 설명 방식을 도입한 것이라고 할 수 있다.

는다고 한 (1ㄷ)을 국어의 음절구조라는 주장이 제기되었다.

　라틴어 기원의 인구어들 그리고 영어, 중국어 등은 (1ㄴ)의 우분지 구조로
보고되어 있다. 이들 언어가 (1ㄴ)의 음절구조라고 하는 근거는 rhyme의 분
지 유무가 실제 음운론적인 현상에 관여적이기 때문이다. 음운론적인 현상
에 해당하는 대표적인 예가 강세 할당이다. 라틴어 기원의 많은 언어들에서
강세(stress) 할당은 중음절이냐 경음절이냐가 관여적인데, 중음절과 경음절
을 구분하는 핵심이 바로 rhyme의 분지 유무이다. 즉 (2)처럼 rhyme이 분지
하지 않은 음절이 경음절이고, (3)처럼 rhyme이 분지한 음절이 중음절이다.
rhyme이 분지하는 양상은 (3ㄱ-ㄹ)처럼 다양하다.

(2)　rhyme

(3)

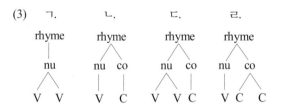

　강세 할당에서 rhyme이 관여적인 예로 라틴어의 강세 할당을 보자. 라틴
어에서 강세는 끝에서 두 번째 음절에 할당된다. 하지만 끝에서 두 번째
음절이 경음절일 때는 끝에서 세 번째 음절에 강세가 할당된다.

(4)[2] ㄱ. refé:cit

ㄴ. reféctus

ㄷ. réficit

(4ㄱ,ㄴ)은 끝에서 두 번째 음절이 중음절이므로 끝에서 두 번째 음절에 강세가 놓인다. 그러나 (4ㄷ)은 rhyme이 분지하지 않은 (2)의 구조인 경음절이다. 그래서 끝에서 세 번째 음절에 강세가 놓인 것을 확인할 수 있다.

경음절이냐 중음절이냐가 강세 할당에 관여적인 것은 영어도 마찬가지이다. (5ㄱ)은 끝에서 세 번째 음절에 강세가 놓였고, (5ㄴ,ㄷ)은 끝에서 두 번째 음절에 강세가 놓여 차이가 있다. 이 차이는 (5ㄱ)의 경우 끝에서 두 번째 음절이 Rhyme이 분지하지 않은 경음절이기 때문이고, (5ㄴ,ㄷ)은 끝에서 두 번째 음절이 Rhyme이 분지한 중음절이기 때문이다.[3]

(5)[4] ㄱ. análysis, cínema, rígorous

ㄴ. horízon, aróma, desírous

ㄷ. agénda, synópsis, moméntous

(4)의 라틴어, (5)의 영어 외에도 많은 언어들에서 경음절/중음절 유무가 강세에 관여적이다. 슬라브어 계통의 폴란드어 역시 2음절어 이상의 단어에서는 끝에서 두 번째 음절에 강세가 놓이지만, 끝에서 두 번째 음절이 경음

2　Allen(1973:51)에서 인용.

3　참고로 (5ㄴ)는 (3ㄱ)의 구조이고, (5ㄷ)은 (3ㄴ)의 구조이다.

4　전상범(2004:382)에서 인용.

절일 때는 끝에서 세 번째 음절에 강세가 놓인다. 그리고 Jakobson(1931:117)에 따르면 고전 아랍어는 단어의 첫 번째 중음절에 강세가 놓였다고 보고하였다.

이상에서 살펴본 라틴어와 라틴어에 뿌리는 둔 인구어들, 영어, 고전 아랍어, 폴란드어 등에서의 강세 현상은 rhyme이 음운론적으로 기능하고 있다는 것을 보여 준다. 그렇기 때문에 이들 언어의 음절구조는 구조적으로 (1ㄴ)의 우분지 구조라고 할 수 있다.

그러면 국어의 음절구조는 (1ㄱ-ㄷ) 중 어느 것일까? 국어의 음절구조가 (1ㄱ-ㄷ) 중 어느 음절구조라고 하려면, 다른 구조가 아닌, 이 구조라고 할 수 있는 음운론적 근거가 제시되어야 한다. 경향성의 높음이라든가 빈도나 비율의 높음 등과 같은 것은 음운론적 근거가 될 수 없다. 왜냐하면 그것은 말 그대로 경향성이나 선호성의 문제일 뿐 구조적인 문제로 인해 야기된 결과가 아니기 때문이다.

국어의 음절구조와 관련한 논의에서는 (1ㄱ)의 삼지적 구조라는 주장(Kim Young-Seok 1984, 박창원 1993, 신승용 2002, 배주채 1996 등), (1ㄴ)의 우분지 구조라는 주장(이기석 1993, Kim Jong-Mi 1986, Sohn 1987 등), (1ㄷ)의 좌분지 구조라는 주장(전상범 1980, 김차균 1987, Ahn 1988, 조성문 2000, 강옥미 2003 등)이 모두 제기되었다. 그런데 국어의 음절구조가 (1ㄴ)이라고 주장하려면, 국어에서 rhyme이 음운론적으로 어떠한 기능을 하고 있다는 것을 증명해야 하고, 마찬가지로 (1ㄷ)이라고 주장하려면 core가 음운론적으로 어떠한 기능을 하고 있는지를 증명해야 한다. 하지만 이용성(1995:129)에서도 지적했듯이 국어의 경우 음절 무게가 관여적인 현상이 거의 없다는 점에서 (1ㄴ)의 우분지 구조를 주장할 만한 자료를 찾기 어렵다. (1ㄷ)의 구조를 주장한 논의들에서는 여러 논거를 제시하기는 하였지만, 모두 경향성과 관련된 것들의 나열에서 나아가지 못하였다. 현재까지는 (1ㄴ)의 우분지 구조를 주장한 논의들에서도, (1ㄷ)의 좌분지 구조를 주장한 논의들에서도 음운론적인 논거나, 구조적인 차원에서의 논거를 제시하지 못하고 있는 상태이다. 단지 경향성과 관련된 현상들을 주로 열거하고 있는 정도인데, 경향성이 높다는 것이 곧 그러한 경향성이 국어의 음절구조를 증언하는 것으로 연결될 수는 없다. 경향성은 구조적인 문제가 아니라 선호성의 문제이기 때문이다.

상대적으로 국어의 음절구조가 (1ㄷ)의 좌분지 구조라고 주장한 논의들이 (1ㄴ)의 우분지 구조라고 주장한 논의들보다 많은데, 좌분지 구조를 주장한 논의들에서 제시한 논거를 정리하면 다음과 같다.

(6)[5] ㄱ. 유아의 언어 습득에서 VC나 CVC 형보다 CV 형이 가장 일반적으로 나타난다(김차균 1987:22).

ㄴ. 발화 실수의 경우, C1VC2에서 C1V나 C2가 치환되는 실수가 가장 많으며 VC2가 치환되는 실수는 거의 나타나지 않는다(문양수 1996: 29).

ㄷ. 말을 빨리 하게 될 때 대체로 '자습서 → 잡서', '태극기 → 택기', '대행진 → 댕진'처럼 CVC에서 CV가 생략된 후 축약된다(전상범 1980:20).

ㄹ. 의성·의태어 등의 중복 현상(reduplication)에서 CV가 복사되는 비율이 가장 높다(Ahn 1988:350).

ㅁ. '소'에 '니은'하면 '손'자가 된다처럼 CV-C로 가르친다(김차균 1987: 23).

---

5   말놀이 현상도 논거로 제시하였지만, 말놀이는 규칙을 정하는 방식에 따라 달라질 수 있기 때문에 언어학적인 증거 자체가 되기 어렵다고 판단하여 제시하지 않는다.

ㅂ. '솔+나무 → 소나무'의 'ㄹ' 탈락(Ahn 1988:351)이나 '만들- + -은 → 만든'의 'ㄹ' 탈락(문양수 1996:42)에서 종성의 자음이 탈락되는데, 이는 국어의 음절구조가 CV-C 구조임을 보여준다.

ㅅ. C1VC2에서 C2는 한 음절 내부나 두 음절 연쇄에서 일어나는 음운현상에 직접적으로 관여하지 못하는데, 이는 음절이 CV-C로 위계화되어 있기 때문이다(문양수 1996, 김주필 1999).

좌분지 구조라는 주장에 대한 비판은 신승용(2002), 이주희(2007)에서 자세히 이루어진 바 있다. 비판 내용을 간략히 정리하면, (6ㄱ-ㅂ)은 구조의 문제라기보다는 경향성이 문제이고, 이러한 경향성은 국어의 특성이 아니라 언어 보편적인 특성이라는 것이다. 즉 언어 보편적으로 CV의 음절형을 지향하는 경향성이 있는데, 이를 굳이 국어 음절구조의 특성이라고 특정할수 없다는 것이다. 예컨대 영어의 음절구조는 우분지 구조이지만 그렇다고 VC 음절의 빈도가 더 높게 나타나지는 않는다. 영어 역시 CV 음절형을 지향하고 CV 음절형의 빈도가 가장 높다.[6] 그러니까 CV 음절형을 지향하는 경향성을 가지고 국어의 음절구조가 좌분지 구조라는 주장을 한다면, 평행하게 영어의 음절구조도 우분지 구조가 아니라 좌분지 구조라고 해야할 것이다. 그러니까 (1ㄱ-ㅂ)이 국어의 음절구조가 좌분지 구조라는 주장의 논거가 될 수 없다.

(6ㅅ)의 경우에도 당장 '달나라 → [달라라]'만 떠올려도 논거가 될 수 없

---

6 언어 현상이 아니라 기억과 관련된 실험으로, Lee Yongeun(2006)은 단기기억실험에서 영어권 청자는 CV보다 VC 패턴을 더 잘 기억하는 반면, 국어 화자는 VC보다 CV 패턴을 더 잘 기억한다고 보고하였다. 하지만 한국어에서 VC 패턴, 영어에서 CV 패턴 역시 예외로만 묵과할 수 없는 수치를 보인다고 하면서, 이는 음절구조의 문제가 아니라 경향성의 문제로 보는 것이 타당하다고 결론 내렸다.

다는 것을 금방 알 수 있다. (1ㅅ)은 '알는 → 아는'의 종성 /ㄹ/ 탈락, 그리고 '굳혀 → [구처]'에서 움라우트의 적용을 막는 것이 두 번째 음절의 'ㅊ' 때문이라는 것 등을 그 근거 현상으로 들었다.[7] 그러나 '달나라, 물놀이, 달님, 별님' 등 순행 유음동화의 경우에는 첫째 음절의 C2가 동화주로 음운 변동에 직접적으로 관여한다. 그래서 (6ㅅ)과 같은 얘기는 국어 전체 음운 변동을 대상으로 한 결론이 아니라, 필요한 음운 변동을 들어서 제시한 것에 지나지 않는다. 만일 김주필(1999:64-65)의 주장대로 국어의 음절구조가 CV-C로 위계화되어 있어서 C1VC2의 C2가 음운 변동에 관여하지 못한다면, 그것은 구조적인 문제이니까 C2가 음운 변동에 관여하는 현상이 존재해서는 안 된다. 하지만 존재한다는 것은 그것이 구조의 문제와는 관계없다는 것을 증언한다.[8]

이주희(2007)는 국어의 음절구조에 대한 논의들을 종합적으로 정리하면서 정작 결론을 내지는 않았다. 그 이유는 제시된 논거들이 모두 음운론적인 논거로 보기 어렵다는 점에서 해당 구조임을 확증적으로 보여 주지 못한다고 판단했기 때문으로 보인다. 그러면서 음운 이론의 방식으로는 결론을 내기 어려우므로 실험을 바탕으로 음절구조를 규명해야 한다는 것으로 논의를 정리하였다. 그런데 실험을 통해서 음절구조를 규명하는 것은 더 어려운 일이다. 실험도 어차피 선호성과 관련된 비율이나 경향성의 정도 이상을

---

7 종성 자음의 탈락은 음절구조가 CV-C로 위계화되어 있기 때문이라는 것이다. 그런데 종성 자음 탈락은 국어의 특수한 현상이 아니라, 우분지 구조인 영어에서 나타나는 현상이다. 만일 종성 자음 탈락이 국어에서만 나타나는 특수한 현상이라면, 생각해 볼 수 있는 논거가 될 수 있을 것이다.

8 언어보편적으로 동화는 순행동화보다 역행동화가 많다고 알려져 있다. C1VC2에서 C2가 음운 변동에 직접 관여하는 경우가 적은 것은 이러한 일반성의 연장선에서 해석하는 것이 맞을 것이다.

말해 줄 수 없을 것이기 때문이다.

　신승용(2002)에서 정리한 것처럼 국어의 음절구조에 대한 논의가 (1ㄴ)의 우분지 구조라는 주장도 제기될 수 있고, (1ㄷ)의 좌분지 구조라는 주장도 제기될 수 있다는 것은 논리적으로 국어의 음절구조가 (1ㄱ)의 삼지적 구조라는 것을 증언한다고 할 수 있다. 우분지 구조와 좌분지 구조는 모순 관계이다. 즉 우분지 구조이면 당연히 좌분지 구조일 수 없고, 좌분지 구조이면 우분지 구조일 수 없다. 그런데 우분지 구조라고 볼 수도 있고, 좌분지 구조라고 볼 수도 있다는 것은 삼지적 구조이어야만 가능하다. 삼지적 구조가 아닌 좌분지 구조나 우분지 구조로는 이러한 양상을 설명할 수 없다.[9]

　실질적인 국어의 음절 이론서라고 할 수 있는 훈민정음에서 국어의 음절은 삼지적 구조임을 분명히 밝히고 있다. 그리고 이러한 음절 분석을 우리는 중국의 운학의 영향을 받았음에도 중국 운학을 단순히 모방하지 않고, 국어에 대한 주체적 분석을 한 결과라고 평가한다. 그러니까 통시적인 관점에서도 훈민정음 이후에 국어의 음절구조가 변화했다는 것을 증명하지 못하는 한, 국어의 음절구조를 삼지적 구조가 아닌, 우분지 구조라든가 좌분지 구조라고 하는 것은 설득력이 없다고 할 것이다.

9　삼지적 구조, 우분지 구조, 좌분지 구조 3개 외에 또 다른 구조가 있다면 우분지 구조일 수도, 좌분지 구조일 수도 없다고 해서 곧 삼지적 구조라고 할 수는 없다. 제3의 구조가 존재하기 때문이다. 하지만 실제 상정될 수 있는 구조가 3개밖에 없다면, 우분지 구조도 아니고 좌분지 구조도 아니거나 또는, 우분지 구조일 수도 있고, 좌분지 구조일 수도 있다는 것은 삼지적 구조일 수밖에 없다.

3. 골격 층렬의 성격과 국어 음절구조에서 골격 층렬

음절이 소위 자립분절 음운론으로 본격적으로 출발한 것은 Kahn(1976)에서부터였다고 할 수 있다. Kahn(1976)의 음절은 음절이 분절음에 직접 연결되는 구조였다.

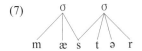

(7)

그런데 (7)은 탈락에 이은 장모음화 현상을 제대로 설명해 주기 어려웠다. 그래서 Clement and Keyser(1983)는 음절 층렬과 분절음 층렬의 사이에 시간 단위라는 골격 층렬을 상정하였다.

음절 층렬과 분절음 층렬 사이에 골격 층렬이 독립적으로 존재한다는 생각은 McCarthy(1979)에서 처음 제안되었다. McCarthy(1979)는 고전 아랍어를 대상으로 [±consonantal] 자질의 CV 음절 형판이 분절음과 독립된 자립분절 단위임을 논증하였다. McCarthy(1979)가 주목한 것은 바로 아랍어의 독특한 어근-어형 형태론의 까다로운 문제였는데, 이를 CVCVC 형판(template)에 어근 형태소를 연결함으로써 해결하였다. 아랍어는 (8)에서 보듯이 형태소라는 구성소가 연속적인 하위 분절음을 이루는 것이 아니라 단어 곳곳에 흩어져 있는 것처럼 나타난다.

(8) ㄱ. 표준구조: daras-a(he studied) rasam-a(he drew)

　　ㄴ. 사역형: darras-a(he taught) rassam-a(he made draw)

　　ㄷ. 명사형: dars-un(a lesson) rasm-un(a drawing)

ㄹ. 행위자형: darraas-un(student) rassaam-un(draftsman)

ㅁ. 분사형: daaris(studing) raasim(drawing)

(8)에서 보면 세 개의 자음 'drs', 'rsm'은 변하지 않고 고정된 순서로 되어 있다. 그리고 어형 변화도 일정한 규칙성을 보인다. 즉 (9ㄱ)에서 보듯이 CVCVC라는 표준 구조에서 (8ㄴ)의 사역형은 CVCCVC, (8ㄷ)의 명사형은 CVCC, (8ㄹ)의 행위자형은 CVCCVVC, (8ㅁ)의 분사형은 CVVCVC의 어간 형태를 취한다. 그리고 첫 번째 모음은 /a/이고 두 번째 모음은 /a/이거나 /i/로 거의 일정하다. 따라서 동일한 형태론적 범주에 속하는 단어들은 최소한 어근 자음과 모음의 상대적 위치를 규정하는 형판에서는 같다고 할 수 있다. 이러한 어형 변화를 어간에 접사를 첨가하는 단선적인 방식으로는 설명하기 어렵다. 이를 McCarthy(1979)는 [±consonantsl] 자질을 자립분절 층렬에 설정하여, CV 형판에 의해 형태론적 범주가 결정되는 것으로 아랍어의 특징을 설명하였다. 이를 도식화하면 (9)와 같다.

(9)   ㄱ he studied   ㄴ he taught   ㄷ student

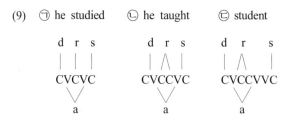

(9)의 도식은 아랍어의 어형 변화가 자음과 모음의 변화에 의해서가 아니라, CV 형판의 변화에 의해서 이루어짐을 분명하게 보여준다. 이처럼 아랍어에서 어형의 형태론적 범주를 결정하는 것은 자음도 모음도 아닌 CV 형판의 구조이다. 이러한 사실을 근거로 McCarthy(1979)는 자음이나 모음과는

독립된 자립적인 단위로서 CV-층렬을 설정하였다.

　Clement and Keyser(1983)에서 CV-층렬의 C, V는 McCarthy(1979)의 C, V와는 본질적으로 다르다. Clement and Keyser(1983)에서 CV-층렬의 C, V는 시간 단위이다. 시간 단위라는 점에서 C와 V는 같고, 단지 결과적으로 C는 [-syllabic], V는 [+syllabic]의 성격을 가진다. Clement and Keyser (1983:8)의 기술을 그대로 옮기면 CV-층렬의 C는 음절의 비정점(non-peak), V는 음절의 정점(peak)을 나타낸다. V가 음절 정점과 연결되므로 소위 성절 자음 'button['bʌtn]'의 두 번째 음절 /n/, 'bottle['bɑ : tl]'의 두 번째 음절 /l/도 V에 연결된다. C이든 V이든 음운론적으로는 시간 단위를 나타낸다는 점에 서는 같기 때문에 CV-층렬 대신 X-층렬이 제안되기도 하였다. X-층렬의 X 역시 시간 단위이다.

　또 다른 음절 이론으로 McCarthy and Prince(1986)는 모라-층렬(mora-tier)을 상정하였다. CV-층렬과 X-층렬이 음절의 무게, 즉 경음절이냐 중음 절이냐의 구분에 초점을 둔 것이라면, 모라 모형은 음절의 양에 초점을 둔 것이다.[10] 모라 음운론에서 모라 역시 음절의 양을 나타내는 것으로 음장과 관련된 단위이다. 이처럼 영어에서 골격 층렬의 골격은 음장과 관련되어 있 다는 사실에서 골격 층렬은 음운론적으로 그 근거가 분명히 있는 존재이다.

　그러면 국어에서도 골격 층렬의 골격이 음운론적 단위인가? 음운론적 단

10　CV-층렬을 비롯한 X-층렬(X-tier) 이론이 분절음의 측면에서 골격에 대한 개념을 발전 시킨 것인데 비해, 모라 이론은 골격에 대해 운율적 개념을 발전시킨 것이다(Kenstowicz 1994:428). 골격 층렬이 시간 단위이지만, 모음 앞의 골격은 시간 단위로서 기능하지 않 는 것이 일반적이다. 모라 이론에서는 골격 층렬이 모라로 이루어져 있고, 모든 음절은 하나의 모라를 가지거나 두 개의 모라를 가지고 있다. 그리고 이 모라의 숫자에 의해 경음절과 중음절이 구분된다. 즉 경음절음은 하나의 모라를 가진 음절이고, 중음절은 두 개의 모라를 가진 음절이다.

위라면 어떤 음운론적 기능을 하는가? 사실 국어에서 음절을 다룬 대부분의 논의들에서 CV-층렬을 상정하면서도, 정작 국어에서 CV-층렬의 C, V가 무엇인지에 대해 논의된 경우가 거의 없다.[11] 그리고 대부분의 논의들에서 C, V는 각각 자음, 모음을 나타내는 기호처럼 사용하고 있다. 그렇기 때문에 음절구조를 다룬 많은 논의들에서 골격 층렬에 분절음 층렬의 활음 /y, w/와 연결되는 G-마디도 상정하고 있다. 하지만 정작 G-마디가 무엇인지에 대한 언급은 없다. G-마디를 상정하는 논의들에서 G는 단지 활음을 나타내는 기호처럼 사용하고 있고, C와 V 역시 단순히 자음, 모음을 나타내는 기호로 사용하고 있다. 이는 음절음운론에서의 골격 층렬의 골격과는 아무런 상관이 없는 기호 사용이다. 앞서도 언급했듯이 골격 층렬은 C와 V로 표시하든, X로 표시하든 음운론적으로는 시간 단위이고, 그래서 C와 V 그리고 X가 시각적으로는 다른 기호이지만 음운론적으로는 동일하다. 그러니까 골격 층렬에 활음 /y, w/와 연결되는 골격 G를 상정하는 것은 이론 내적으로 아무런 근거가 없는 것이라고 하겠다.

사실 국어의 음절구조를 다룬 논의들에서 골격 층렬의 음운론적 실체가 무엇인지에 대한 논의가 거의 없었다. 영어를 비롯한 인구어에서는 골격 층렬이 무게 또는 양과 관련된, 분절음과 독립된 단위로서 그 음운론적인 기능을 확인할 수 있다. 평행하게 국어의 음절구조에서 골격 층렬을 상정하려면, 음운론적으로 그것이 어떤 기능을 하는지에 대한 논증이 있어야 한다. C, V, G가 자음, 모음, 활음을 나타내는 표지 기호라고 한다면, 굳이 골격 층렬이 따로 필요 없고, Kahn(1976)의 (7)과 같은 구조로도 충분하다.

이와 관련하여 국어에서도 골격 층렬이 시간 단위일 가능성은 없는가?

---

11   이하에 국어의 골격 층렬을 언급할 때는 기본적으로 CV-층렬을 가정하고 기술한다.

(10) ㄱ. 마음 → 맘[맘ː], 노을 → 놀[놀ː]

ㄴ. 게임 → [겜], 내일 → [낼], 무얼 → [뭘], 그리고 → [글고]

(10ㄱ)의 보상적 장모음화 예를 통해서 골격 층렬의 골격을 시간 단위라고 한다면, 그것은 현재라는 공시태에서는 적어도 과잉일반화이다. 현재는 (10ㄱ)처럼 장음으로 발음하는 것이 오히려 예외적이라고 해야 하는 상황이다. 당장 (10ㄴ)만 하더라도 장모음화가 일어나지 않고, 젊은 세대에서는 (10ㄱ)도 단음으로 발음하기도 하기 때문이다.[12] (10ㄴ)의 경우는 음장이 변별적 기능을 하고 있는 경상도의 경우에도 젊은 세대 발음에서 장음화된 발음을 듣기가 매우 어렵다.

그러면 골결 층렬이 음운론적으로 아무런 기능도 하지 않는 것인가? 음운이 물리적인 실재에 기반하고 있지만, 물리적인 실재가 곧 음운은 아니다. 즉 물리적인 실재와 인식적 실재가 일치하는 경우가 대부분이지만, 그렇지 않은 경우도 있다. 그런 점에서 음운은 물리적인 실재이면서 동시에 심리적인 실재이기도 하다. 이러한 관점의 연장에서 국어 화자에게서 골격 층렬의 골격도 심리적 실재로서, 음운론적인 기능을 하는 단위로 볼 여지는 없을까?

---

12 신승용(2002:235)에서는 (10ㄱ) 때문에 V가 시간 단위로서의 기능도 갖는다고 보았다. 하지만 (10ㄱ)이 시간 단위의 증거라고 하기에는 그렇지 않은 현상들이 더 일반적이기 때문에 시간 단위로 일반화할 수 없다. '으' 탈락, '아/어' 탈락이 보상적 장모음화를 수반하지 않고, 현재 젊은 세대에서 새로이 만들어진 공시적인 축약의 경우에는 (10ㄴ)처럼 장모음화를 수반하지 않기 때문이다.

(11)

	어간 말음절의 상태		
	자음으로 끝날 때		모음으로 끝날 때
조사	-이	~	-가
	-을	~	-를
	-은	~	-는
어미	-으X	~	-X

신승용(2002:233-234)에서 언급했듯이 (11)에서 이형태 선택은 자음의 종류나 모음의 종류와는 무관하다. 단지 선행 어간 말음절이 모음으로 끝나느냐 자음으로 끝나느냐와만 관련이 있다.[13] 그리고 모음 뒤의 자음이 한 개이냐 두 개이냐도 관여적이지 않다. 이러한 사실은 (11)의 선택이 분절음 차원에서 분절음에 민감한 것이라기보다는 음절의 구조에 민감하다는 것을 말해 준다.

국어 화자라면 누구나 음절에 대한 인식과 함께 음절 위치에 대한 인식을 뚜렷이 갖고 있다. 직관적으로 모음을 중심으로 모음은 중성, 모음의 앞쪽은 초성, 모음의 뒤쪽은 종성이라고 인식한다. 이러한 음절 위치에 대한 인식은 McCarthy(1979)의 C, V와 평행한 개념이지만, 같지는 않다. McCarthy(1979)의 C, V는 [±consonantsl]과 일치하지만, 국어에서 V-마디(V-node)는 정확히 모음과 일치하는 개념이 아니고, C-마디 역시 정확히 자음과 일치하는 개념은 아니다. (12ㄱ)처럼 분지하는 V, (12ㄴ)처럼 분지하는 C가 존재하기 때문이다.[14]

---

13   한 분 심사위원의 지적처럼 어미 '-으X ~ -X' 교체의 경우 정확히는 /ㄹ/을 제외한 자음과 '/ㄹ/과 모음 뒤'라고 해야 한다. 여기서는 단지 큰 틀에서 보면 자음으로 끝나느냐 모음으로 끝나느냐가 핵심이고, 이 틀 안에서 /ㄹ/이 예외적이라고 해석하고자 한 것이다.

14   음장의 대립이 있는 세대나 지역의 경우 장모음이 두 개의 V-칸에 연결된 것으로 본다

(12)　ㄱ.　　　　ㄴ.

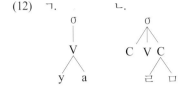

V가 분지하든 아니든 중성이고, C가 분지하든 아니든 종성이다. 즉 국어 화자는 /a/도 중성이라고 인식하고, /ya/도 중성이라고 인식한다. 평행하게 '살'의 /ㄹ/도 종성이라고 인식하고, '삶'의 /ㄲ/도 종성이라고 인식한다. 그렇기 때문에 (11)의 이형태 교체 조건에서 V의 분지 유무나 C의 분지 유무는 상관이 없다. 단지 C로 끝나느냐 아니냐 즉, 종성이 있느냐 없느냐만이 관여적이다. 이는 음절핵인 중성을 중심으로 앞쪽은 초성, 뒤쪽은 종성으로 인식하는 인식적 실재로서의 단위가 음운론적으로 실재한다고 보아야 하는 근거로 볼 수 있다. 이처럼 국어에서 골격 층렬의 C, V는 한 음절 내부에서 음절초, 음절핵, 음절말이라는 상대적 위치에 대한 인식적 실재로서 음운론적 기능을 한다고 할 수 있다.

공시적인 사실에 기반한 직접적인 증거는 아니지만, 훈민정음의 창제 과정 자체도 음절을 '초성-중성-종성'으로 구분한 뒤에, 초성에 오는 소리, 중성에 오는 소리, 종성에 오는 소리에 대해 각각 문자를 창제하였다.[15] 종성

면, V는 시간 단위의 기능이 일부 있다고 할 수도 있다. 그렇지만 음절의 관점에서 보면, 초분절 단위로서 음장의 변별적 기능은 골격 층렬의 C, V와는 별도의 방식으로 설명해야 하지 않나 하는 생각도 있다. 현재로서는 '어떻게'에 대해 말할 정도는 아니기에, 단지 가설 정도 수준에서의 얘기이다.

15　음절의 초성, 중성, 종성에 대한 인식과 관련된 기술 한두 가지를 더 언급하면 다음과 같다. '자의 요체는 중성이고 초성, 종성과 합해서 음을 이룬다(盖字韻之要 在於中聲 初終合而成音<制字解>)'든가, '중성만으로 음절을 이룰 수 있다(中聲可得成音<終聲解>)'는 진술에서 음절을 초성, 중성, 종성으로 삼분하고, 음절의 각 위치에 대한 분절 인식이 명확

에는 다시 초성을 쓴다는 '終聲復用初聲'도 초성, 종성이라는 음절 위치에 대한 명확한 인식에 기반한 진술이다. 이 역시 분절음과 음절 사이를 연결하는 '초성-중성-종성'의 위치에 대한 인식적 실재로서의 단위가 존재한다고 보는 것을 뒷받침해 준다.

골격 층렬과 관련된 또 하나의 문제는 국어의 음절구조를 다룬 논의들에서 상정하고 있는 골격 층렬의 G-마디이다. 이들 논의에서 'ㅑ/ya/'는 (12ㄱ)이 아니라, (13)처럼 설명한다.

(13)

무엇보다 (13)의 문제는 G-마디라는 것이 이론 내적으로 아무런 근거가 없다는 점이다. 골격 층렬에 G-마디를 상정하는 것은 골격 층렬의 C, V를 단선 음운론의 연장선에서 자음과 모음으로 이해하기 때문에 생긴 것이라고 할 수밖에 없다. 그러니까 활음을 나타내는 기호로 G를 설정할 수 있는 것이다. 하지만 CV-음운론에서 골격 층렬의 C-마디와 V-마디가 각각 자음과 모음이 아닌데, 단지 활음을 나타내는 G-마디를 상정하는 것은 당연히 이론 내적으로 근거가 없다. 이는 복선 음운론의 바탕 위에 단선 음운론을 섞어 놓은 것과 다르지 않다고 할 것이다.

음운 현상을 통해서 볼 때도 골격 층렬에 G-마디를 상정할 근거는 없다. (14)는 일상의 자연스러운 발화에서 빈번하게 일어나는 활음 탈락이다. 그

하였음을 확인할 수 있다.

런데 (14)에서 활음이 탈락했다는 것은 (15)에서의 자음 탈락과 달리 언중들이 잘 인식하지 못하는 경향이 있다.

(14) ㄱ. 계속 → [kyesok~kesok], 폐단 → [pyedan~pedan]

ㄴ. 봐라 → [pwara~para], 뭐 → [mwə~mə]

(15) ㄱ. [아니, 아시니]

ㄴ. [노으니, 노아]

(15ㄱ)에서 /ㄹ/ 탈락, (15ㄴ)에서 /ㅎ/ 탈락을 인식하지 못하는 화자는 없다. 그러나 (14)에서 /y, w/ 탈락은 주의 깊게 들으라고 해야 활음이 탈락했음을 겨우 인지하는 경향이 있다. 특히 (16)의 경우에는 /y/가 탈락한 발음을 듣고도 /y/가 탈락했다고 인식하지 못할 뿐만 아니라, 스스로 /y/가 탈락한 발음을 하면서도 /y/가 탈락하지 않은 발음을 하고 있다고 우기는 경우까지 있다.

(16) 가져[katʃə], 쳐[tʃʰə], 쪄[tʃˀə]

그러면 자음 탈락과 달리 왜 활음 탈락에 대한 인식은 상대적으로 약할까? 이는 활음과 연결되는 골격이 골격 층렬에 따로 존재하지 않기 때문이다. 즉 활음은 (12ㄱ)처럼 V-마디, 즉 중성에 연결된다. 그렇기 때문에 활음이 탈락하더라도 중성인 V는 여전히 그대로 있기 때문에 자음 탈락과 달리 상대적으로 인식하기가 어려운 것이다. 반면 자음 탈락은 골격 층렬의 C가 탈락하기 때문에 명확하게 인식할 수 있다.

자음이나 모음의 탈락은 이와 연결된 골격 층렬의 골격도 탈락하여 음절에서의 변화를 바로 파악할 수 있다. 골격 층렬의 C-마디나 V-마디의 탈락은 음절의 구조 자체를 변화시키므로, 당연히 탈락에 대해 민감하게 인식하게 된다. 하지만 활음의 경우 활음과 연결된 골격 층렬의 골격이 따로 없다. 그렇기 때문에 활음이 탈락하더라도 골격 층렬에는 변화가 없고, 골격 층렬에 변화가 없기 때문에 음절의 구조에는 변화가 없다. 이러한 까닭에 상대적으로 자음, 모음과 달리 활음은 탈락하더라도 탈락에 대한 인식이 약할 수밖에 없다.

물론 자음 탈락의 경우에도 '아니'에서의 /ㄹ/ 탈락과, '놓으니[노으니]'에서의 /ㅎ/ 탈락의 인식 정도가 다르다고 할 수 있다. 이러한 인지상의 미시적인 차이까지 여기서 고려하지는 못한다.

4. 활음의 음절구조상에서의 위치

국어에서 활음은 음운이냐 아니냐 하는 것부터 논란이 된 적이 있다. 강창석(1989:23-24), 정연찬(1991:382)에서는 /y/, /w/를 독립된 음소로 보지 않고, 각각 /i/, /u/(또는 /o/)의 조건 변이음으로 해석하였다. 그 근거는 훈민정음 창제 당시부터 활음에 대한 문자 배당의 마련이 없었고, 활음 /y/, /w/가 각각 모음 /i/, /u/(또는 /o/)와 상보적 분포를 이룬다고 보아 독립된 음소로의 설정을 반대하였다.[16]

---

16 이에 대해 신승용(1998:27)에서 첫째, 음운론의 대상이 문자가 아니라는 점, 둘째, 상보적 분포를 이룬다고 해서 모두 변이음 관계는 아니라는 점, 셋째, '가구(/kaku/)'와 '야구(/yaku/)'의 의미 차는 /k/와 /y/에 의해 변별된다는 점에서 활음이 음소임을 다시 한번 분명히 하였다.

그런데 강창석(1989)에서 말하는 상보적 분포 환경이라는 것은 국어에서 활음이 독립해서 음절을 이루지 못한다는 특성을 기술한 것에 다름 아니다. 왜냐하면 음소배열상으로는 '주안상/ʧuansaŋ/', '좌석/ʧwasək/'에서 보듯이 동일한 조건환경인 /ʧ/와 /a/ 사이에 /w/, /u/가 모두 올 수 있기 때문이다. 그러니까 음소배열상으로는 상보적 분포가 아니다.

음절구조와 관련하여 활음이 논란이 되는 부분은 활음 /y, w/가 음절핵 요소이냐 아니냐이다. 활음의 음절구조상에서의 위치는 언어마다 차이가 있다. 또한 동일한 언어를 대상으로도 논란이 되는 주제이기도 한데, 특히 논란이 되는 것은 상향 이중모음의 활음, 즉 모음에 선행하는 활음의 위치이다.

영어에서는 모음에 선행하는 활음은 음절초 요소로 보는 것이 일반적이다(Kenstowicz 1994:258). 그리고 모음에 후행하는 활음은 모음과 함께 하향 이중모음을 구성하는 것으로 즉, 음절핵에 연결된 요소로 보지만, 음절말 요소로 해석하는 견해도 없지는 않다. 영어에서 모음 앞의 활음이 음절초 요소라는 현상적인 증거로 Ahn(1988:335)은 관사 'a'와 'an'의 결합 양상을 들었다. 자음 앞에서는 'a', 모음 앞에서는 'an'이 결합하는데, 'a year', 'a youth'에서 보듯이 /y/ 앞에서 'a'가 결합하여 /y/가 자음과 같은 행동을 한다. 이는 'a wind', 'a willow'에서 보듯이 /w/의 경우도 마찬가지이다(Hogg and McCully 1987:39). /y, w/가 관사와의 결합에서 자음과 같은 행동을 한다는 것은 /y, w/가 자음과 마찬가지로 음절초 요소임을 말해 준다는 것이다.

영어에서 모음에 선행하는 활음을 음절초 요소로 보게 되는 결정적 이유는 모음에 선행하는 활음의 존재 유무가 중음절을 결정하는 데 관여적이지 않기 때문이다. 중음절은 rhyme이 분지하는 음절인데, 상향 이중모음이 중음절을 이루지 못한다는 것은 상향 이중모음의 /y, w/를 음절핵 요소로 볼 수 없게 한다. 그래서 영어에서 모음에 선행하는 활음은 음운론적으로 음절

초 요소로 보는 것이 여타의 현상을 설명하는 데 더 유리한 면이 있다.[17]

프랑스어의 경우에 Kaye and Lowenstamm(1984)은 모음 앞의 활음이 (17ㄱ), (17ㄴ)의 두 가지 방식으로 연결된다고 보고하고 있다. (17ㄱ,ㄴ)을 음절구조로 나타낸 것이 (18ㄱ,ㄴ)이다.

(17) ㄱ. les watts[lewat]

les westerns[lewestern]

ㄴ. les oies[lezwa]

les oints[lezwɛ̃]

(18) ㄱ. watt ㄴ. oie

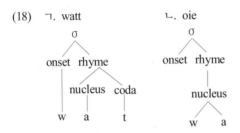

(17ㄱ)에서는 'les'의 's'가 탈락하는 데 반해, (17ㄴ)에서는 'les'의 's[z]'가 연음된다. 그 이유를 (17ㄱ)에서는 활음 /w/가 음절초에 위치하기 때문이고, (17ㄴ)에서는 /w/가 음절핵에 위치하기 때문으로 해석한 것이다. 이에 따르면 프랑스어의 경우 모음에 선행하는 활음의 음절구조상에서의 위치는 고정된 것이 아니라, 맥락에 따라 음절초에 연결되는지 음절핵에 연결되는

---

17 반면 하향 이중모음은 중음절인데, 이는 모음에 후행하는 활음, 즉 하향 이중모음의 활음이 음절핵 요소임을 보여 주는 증거가 된다.

지가 결정된다.

중국어에서도 모음(핵음)에 선행하는 활음의 음절구조상에서의 위치가 논란이 되는 주제이다. 孫景濤(2006:45)는 모음 앞의 활음이 음절에 직접 연결되는 단위로 해석하였는데, 이는 모음 앞의 활음을 음절핵 요소로 보지 않는 것이다. 반면 Lin Yen-Hwei(2010:169)는 모음에 선행하는 활음은 음절초 요소로, 모음에 후행하는 활음은 모음과 함께 음절핵의 요소로 보았다. 또 다른 견해로 엄익상(2013)은 모음에 선행하는 활음은 음절초 요소로, 모음에 후행하는 활음은 음절말 요소로 해석하였다. 아무튼 중국어의 경우 모음에 선행하는 활음은 음절초에 연결되는 요소로 해석하는 것이 우세하다.

국어에서도 모음에 선행하는 활음, 즉 상향 이중모음의 활음이 음절초 요소인지, 음절핵 요소인지에 대해 논란이 있다. Lee Byung-Gun(1982), 김차균(1987), Ahn(1988), 엄태수(1996), 강옥미(2003) 등에서는 음절초 요소로 보았다. 반면 Kim-Renaud(1978), Kim Jong-Mi(1986), Sohn(1987), 이동화(1998) 등에서는 음절핵 요소로 보았다.

먼저 상향 이중모음의 활음이 음절초 요소라는 주장의 논거로 Ahn(1988: 334-335)은 5가지를 제시하였는데, 국어와 직접적으로 관련된 음운론적인 논거는 한 가지뿐이다.[18] (19)의 호격 조사 교체가 바로 그것이다.

---

18 모두 6가지를 제시하였는데, 하나는 모음 뒤의 활음 즉, 하향 이중모음의 활음에 대한 것이다. 상향 이중모음의 활음이 음절초 요소라는 증거로 제시한 다른 4가지는 다음과 같다. ㉠ 활음은 다른 자음과 마찬가지로 빠르게 위치를 이동한다. ㉡ 영어에서 부정관사가 활음 앞에서는 자음 앞과 마찬가지로 'a'가 온다. ㉢ 언어보편적으로 활음은 모음이나 성절 자음과 구분된다. ㉣ 말놀이에서 활음은 복사되지 않는다.

(19)

	자음 뒤	모음 뒤
ㄱ.	상순-아	철수-야
ㄴ.	하늘-아	나무-야

호격 조사 '-아 ~ -야'의 이형태 선택 조건은 선행하는 어간이 자음으로 끝나느냐 모음으로 끝나느냐이다. 이때 모음 어간 뒤에서 '-야'가 오는 것은 모음충돌회피로 설명된다. 만일 /y/가 모음이라면 모음충돌이 회피되었다고 볼 수 없으므로 /y/가 음절초 요소로 보아야 한다는 것이다.

상향 이중모음의 활음이 음절초 요소라는 또 다른 증거로 신승용(1998)은 'ㅈyV → ㅈV'에서의 /y/ 탈락, 'pwa → pa'에서의 /w/ 탈락을 들었다. 이는 /y, w/를 음절초 요소라고 할 때 필수굴곡원리[19]로 더 타당하게 설명할 수 있다는 것이다. 활음이 음절핵 요소라면, 음절초와 음절핵 간에 필수굴곡원리가 작용했다고 해야 하는데, 이는 음절초 내에서 필수굴곡원리가 작용했다고 하는 것보다 유표적이기 때문이다.

그런데 위에서 제시된, 활음이 음절초 요소라는 논거들은 활음이 모음이 아니라는 증거인 것은 분명하다. 그렇지만 이들 논거가 활음이 음절초 요소임을 말해 주는 적극적인 증거라고 보기는 어렵다. 왜냐하면 활음이 모음이 아니기 때문에 활음이 음절핵 요소라고 하더라도 모음충돌은 회피했다고 할 수 있기 때문이다. 그리고 'ㅈyV → ㅈV'에서의 /y/ 탈락, 'pwa → pa'에서의 /w/ 탈락 역시 활음이 음절핵 요소라고 해서 설명이 불가능한 것은 아니다. 이것이 음절구조 내에서의 음절구조제약인지, 음운 연쇄상에서의

---

19 필수굴곡원리는 Leben(1973)에서 제안된 것으로, 운율 층위에서 동일 요소의 인접을 저지하는 현상을 원리화한 것이다.

음운 간의 연결 제약인지 분명하게 말하기 어렵기 때문이다.

활음이 음절핵 요소라는 주장은 Kim-Renaud(1978), Kim Jong-Mi(1986), Sohn(1987), 이동화(1998) 등에서 제기되었다. Kim Jong-Mi(1986)는 국어의 경우 복합 음절초를 허용하지 않는데, 활음이 음절초에 온다고 하면 이러한 국어의 음절구조제약을 어긴다는 점을 지적하였다. 그런데 복합 음절초를 허용하지 않는 것은 순수 자음 연쇄인 경우이고, 활음을 포함한 '자음-활음'의 음절초 연쇄는 별도로 논의될 수 있는 성격이라는 점에서 이것이 적극적인 증거가 되기는 어렵다. 사실이 활음이 음절핵 요소라는 주장은 특별히 많이 제기되지 않았는데, 이는 당연히 그렇다는 인식이 저변에 있었기 때문으로 보인다.

'ㅑ, ㅕ, ㅛ, ㅠ'를 하나의 단위로 즉, 하나의 중성으로 다룬 것은 훈민정음에서 이미 분명히 확인할 수 있다. 훈민정음에서 'ㅑ, ㅕ, ㅛ, ㅠ'는 기본자 11자 중의 하나이고, 그 음운론적 특성은 '起於ㅣ'로 기술하고 있다. '起於ㅣ'라는 것은 곧 /y/로 시작하는 이중모음을 설명한 것에 다름 아니다. 그런데 그러한 특성의 소리를 하나의 자(字)인 'ㅑ, ㅕ, ㅛ, ㅠ'에 대당시킨 것은 /ya, yə, yo, yu/를 하나의 단위 즉, 하나의 중성으로 보았기 때문이다. 당시에 활음을 별도의 음운으로 인식했든 인식하지 못 했든 /ya, yə, yo, yu/를 하나의 자(字)에 대당시킴으로써, 당시는 물론이고 현재에도 'ㅑ, ㅕ, ㅛ, ㅠ'를 중성에 오는 하나의 단위로 인식하게 된 것이다. 중성을 이루는 하나의 단위는 하나의 음운일 수도 있고, 둘 이상의 음운일 수도 있다. 2장에서 골격 층렬의 V가 중성에 대한 인식을 나타내는 단위라고 하였다. 그리고 이 V는 단모음 하나와 연결된 V도 있고, '활음-모음'과 연결된 V도 있다. 그러니까 'ㅑ, ㅕ, ㅛ, ㅠ'를 하나의 단위로 인식한다는 것은 골격 층렬에서 하나의 골격, V-마디로 인식한다는 것이지, 분절음 층렬의 하나의 모음처럼 인식한다는 것은 아니다. 이는 훈민정음에서도 확인할 수 있다. 훈민정음 해례 중 성해에서 중성에 오는 요소는 기본자 11자 외에도 '二字合用字', 'ㅣ相合者' 도 있다.[20] 이들 각각의 경우 음운의 개수가 다르다고 기술하고 있으면서도, 모두 중성에 온다는 점에서는 같다고 본 것이다.

  이러한 인식은 국어의 표기법과 관련이 있다. 활음 /y/, /w/를 표기하는 문자가 따로 존재하지 않기 때문에 일반 언중들이 활음을 떼어내서 하나의 음운으로 인식하기는 쉽지 않다. 그러나 /ya/가 /a/처럼 소리가 하나이냐고 물었을 때 하나라고 대답하는 사람도 찾기 어렵다. 이는 'ㅑ'를 하나의 중성 으로 인식하지만, 그렇다고 하나의 단모음으로 인식하는 것은 아님을 말해 준다.[21]

  결론적으로 국어에서 상향 이중모음의 활음은 모음과 함께 중성에 연결 된다. 훈민정음을 창제할 당시의 국어의 음절 분석이 잘못 이루어졌다고 하지 않는 한 상향 이중모음은 (12ㄱ)과 같은 구조이다. 그렇기 때문에 하나 의 단위 즉, 하나의 중성으로 인식하는 경향이 있는 것이다. 하나의 단위로 인식한다는 것이 곧 하나의 모음으로 인식한다는 것은 당연히 아니다.

---

20 '二字合用字'는 'ㅘ, ㅝ, ㆇ, ㆊ' 4개이고, 'ㅣ相者'는 다시 一字中聲之與ㅣ相合者 10개(ㆎ, ㅐ, ㅚ, ㅟ …), 二字中聲之與ㅣ相合者 4개(ㅙ, ㅞ …)이다. 이들은 모두 2자 이상이라고 하였으므로 2개 이상의 음운의 연쇄라는 것을 인식하고 있었다고 보는 것이 맞다.

21 이지수·박인규(2018)는 고등학생을 대상으로 한 설문조사를 바탕으로 'ㅑ, ㅕ, ㅛ, ㅠ' 를 하나의 모음처럼 인식한다고 주장하기도 하였다. 고등학생 30명을 대상으로 'ㅛ:ㅗ' 3쌍(교수:고수, 교문:고문, 요리:오리), 'ㅕ:ㅓ' 2쌍(겨울:거울, 볏:벗)을 주고 음운의 개수 를 물었는데, 'ㅛ, ㅕ'를 'ㅗ, ㅓ'와 같이 하나로 세었다는 것을 근거로 'ㅛ, ㅑ'가 하나의 음운이라는 주장으로까지 나아갔다. 이 실험은 상향 이중모음을 하나의 단위로 인식한 다는 것을 보여 주는 것은 맞다. 그러나 그렇다고 'ㅛ, ㅕ'가 단모음임을 증명하는 실험 은 아니다.

5. 결론

　지금까지 음절구조의 유형, 음절 층렬과 분절음 층렬 사이의 골격 층렬의 실체, 그리고 음절구조에서 활음의 위치, 이렇게 세 가지 주제에 대해 살펴보았다. 이들 세 가지는 언어마다 차이가 있기 때문에, 음운체계의 차이와 마찬가지로 언어 간의 특성을 살펴보는 것이 국어의 음절을 이해하는 데 도움이 된다. 이런 관점에서 다른 언어들에서 이들 세 가지가 어떤 양상으로 또는 어떤 특성을 가지고 있는지를 살펴보고, 이를 참고하여 국어에서 이들 세 가지가 어떻게 나타나지를 고찰하였다. 논의를 정리하면서 결론을 대신한다.

　첫째, 국어의 음절구조에 대해 우분지 구조라는 주장, 좌분지 구조라는 주장, 삼지적 구조라는 주장이 모두 제기되었다. 이론적으로 상정 가능한 세 가지 음절구조가 모두 제기될 수 있다는 것은 국어의 음절구조가 삼지적 구조임을 증언한다. 좌분지 구조와 우분지 구조는 모순인데, 둘 다 가능하다는 주장이 나올 수 있다는 것은 삼지적 구조가 아니면 불가능하다.

　둘째, 영어나 인구어와 달리 현대국어에서는 골격 층렬의 골격이 시간 단위로 볼 수 있는 현상이 없다. 하지만 국어 화자의 경우 영어나 인구어 화자와 달리 모음을 중심으로 모음은 중성, 모음 앞은 초성, 모음 뒤는 종성이라는 명확한 위치 인식이 있다. 국어에서 골격 층렬의 C-마디, V-마디는 바로 이러한 음절 위치에 대한 인식을 반영하는 인식적 실재이다. 그렇기 때문에 골격 층렬에 G-마디를 상정하는 것은 이론 내적으로도 근거가 없고, 현상적으로도 근거가 없다. 이는 단지 골격 층렬과 분절음 층렬을 구분하지 않는 단선 음운론적 사고의 연장이다.

　셋째, 활음의 음절구조상에서의 위치는 언어마다 차이가 있는데, 국어의 음절구조에서 상향 이중모음의 활음은 모음과 함께 중성에 연결된다. /a/와 /ya/가 동일하게 중성이라고 인식한다는 것은 모음에 선행하는 활음이 중성의 요소라고 할 때에만 설명 가능하다. 현상적으로 호격 조사 '-아~-야'의 이형태 교체나, 'ㅈyV' 연쇄 제약 등은 활음이 모음이 아니라는 증거임에는 분명하지만, 그렇다고 활음이 음절초 요소임을 말해 주는 적극적인 증거는 아니다.

참고문헌

강옥미(2003), 한국어 음운론, 태학사.

강창석(1989), "현대국어 음운론의 허와 실," 국어학 19, 국어학회, 3-40.

김종훈(1989), "영어의 음절구조와 그 조건," 영어영문학 35(3), 한국영어영문학회, 589-608.

김주필(1999), "국어의 음절 내부 구조와 음운 현상," 애산학보 23, 애산학회, 45-72.

김차균(1987), "국어의 음절 구조와 음절핵 안에 일어나는 음운론적 과정," 말 12, 연세대학교 한국어학당, 25-70.

문양수(1996), "음절이론과 국어의 음절구조," 음성학과 언어학, 서울대출판부, 26-49.

박창원(1993), "현대 국어 의성 의태어의 형태와 음운," 새국어생활 3(2), 국립국어연구원, 16-53.

배주채(1996), 국어음운론 개설, 신구문화사.

신승용(1998), "음절화와 활음(/y, w/)의 음운론적 성격에 관하여," 서강어문 14, 서강어문학회, 21-52.

신승용(2002), "한국어의 음절구조," 시학과언어학 4, 시학과언어학회, 294-329.

엄익상(2013), "표준중국어 음절구조와 활음의 위치," 중국언어연구 44, 한국중국언어학회, 41-64.

엄태수(1996), "현대국어의 이중모음화 현상에 대하여," 언어 21, 언어학회, 401-420.

이기석(1993), 음절구조와 음운원리, 한신문화사.

이동화(1998), 최근 이론 중심의 국어음운론, 문창사.

이용성(1995), "음절구조론," 외대논총 13, 부산외국어대학교, 93-142.

이주희(2007), "한국어의 음절구조에 대한 연구 경향과 전망," 한국언어문학 61, 한국언어문학회, 57-81.

이지수·박인규(2018), "반모음 교체 현상에 대한 문법 교육적 기술 방안 연구: 문법 교과서 '모음 축약' 기술에 대하여," 국제어문 78, 국제어문학회, 131-152.

전상범(1980), "Lapsus linguae의 음운론적 해석," 언어 5(2), 한국언어학회, 15-32.

전상범(2004), 음운론, 서울대학교출판부.

정연찬(1991), "현대 국어 이중모음 체계를 다시 생각해 본다," 석정이승욱선생회갑 기념논총, 379-402.

조성문(2000), 국어 자음의 음운 현상에 대한 원리와 제약, 한국문화사.

Ahn, Sang-Cheol (1988), "A Revised Theory of Syllable Phonology," *The Korean Journal of Linguistics* 13(2), The Linguistic Society of Korea, 333-362.

Allen, W. S. (1973), "Accent and Rhythm, Prosodic Features of Latin and Greek: A Study in Theory and Reconstruction," *Cambridge Studies in Linguistics* 12, Cambridge University Press.

Chomsky, N. and Halle, M. (1968), *The sound pattern of English*, New York: Harper.

Clement, G.N. and S.J. Keyser (1983), *CV Phonology: A Generative Theory of the Syllable*, MIT Press.

Fuge (1987), "Branching structure within the syllable," *Journal of Linguistics* 23, 359-377.

Hulst, H. van der and N. Smith (1982), *The Structure of Phonological Representation*, Dordrecht-Holland: Foris Publictions.

Hogg, R. and C.B. McCully (1987), *Metrical Phonology*, Cambridge University Press.

Jakobson, R. (1931), "Die Betonnung und ihre Rolle in der Word-und Syntagmaphonologie," *Travaux du Cercle Linguistique de Prague* Ⅳ, Reprinted in Roman Jakobson, *Selected Writing* Ⅰ, The Haue: Mouton, 117-136.

Kahn, D. (1976), *Syllable based Generalizations in English Phonology*, MIT Ph.D., Distributted by Indiana University Linguistics Club.

Kaye, J. and J. Lowenstamm (1984), "De la syllabicité," In F. Dell, H. Hirst and J-R. Vergnaud eds, *Forme sonore du langage*, Paris: Hermannm 123-159.

Kenstowicz, M. (1994), *Phonology in Generative Grammar*, Blackwell.

Kim, Jong-Mi (1986), *Phonology and Syntax of Korean Morphology*, Ph.D. dessertation, University of Southern California.

Kim-Renaud, Young-Key (1978), "The syllable in Korean phonology," *Papers in Korean linguistics*, ed. by Chin-W. Kim, Columbia, SC: Hombeam press, 85-98.

Kim, Young-Seok (1984), Aspects of Korean Morphology, Ph.D. dissertation,

University of Texas.

Leben, W. (1973), Suprasegmental phonology, Cambridge, MIT Ph.D. dissertation.

Lee, Byung-Gun (1982), "A well-formedness condition on syllable structure," *Linguistics in the Mornning calm*, ed. by I. Y. Yang, Hanshin Publishing Co, 3-91.

Lee, Yen-Hwei (2007), *The Sounds of Chinese*, Cambridge Universtiy Press.

Lee, Yongeun (2006), *Sub-syllabic constituency in Korean and English*, Ph.D. dissertation, Northwestern University.

Levin, J. (1985), *A metrical Theory of syllabicity*, MIT Ph.D dissertation.

McCarthy, J. (1979), *Formal problems in Semitic phonology and morphology*, Ph.D. dissertation, MIT.

McCarthy and Prince (1986), *Prosodic Morphology*, Waltham MA: Brandeis University, ms.

Selkirk, E.O. (1982), "The syllable," In Hulst, H. van der and N. Smith(1982), *The Structure of Phonological Representation* Ⅱ, 337-383.

Sohn, Hyang-Sook (1987), *Underspecification in Korean Phonology*, Ph.D. dissertation, University of Illinois at Urbana Champagne.

孫景濤(2006), 介音在音節中的地位, 言語科學 21, 44-52.

독일어 관용구에서 파생된 조어에 대한 고찰

정수정

1. 서론

언어는 정적인 것이 아니라, 생성과 성장 그리고 소멸의 과정을 겪으며 변화하는 동적인 기호이다. 이러한 언어변화는 다양한 동인에 의해 이루어진다. 언어변화의 동인에는 우선 시간상의 절약과 편리함을 위하여 축소된 형태의 언어를 사용하는 언어경제성과 새로운 환경변화에 대한 기존 어휘 목록의 부족으로 인한 혁신을 들 수 있다. 또한 의사소통의 조건이나 목적에 따라 언어수단을 선택하는 데에 화자의 유연한 태도에 의해 발생하는 변이도 이에 속한다.

관용구 Phraseologismus는 두 개 이상의 어휘로 이루어진 관습적인 어휘 결합체로 한 언어의 어휘목록의 기본 단위다(정수정 2019:2). 이 관용구가 조어 Wortbildung의 기저가 되어 형성된 어휘들이 있다. 조어는 원래 기존의 단어나 형태소를 토대로 해당언어의 어휘 형성 원리에 맞게 만들어진 새로운 어휘다. 사실 이러한 조어 형성 원리는 어린이의 어휘 습득과정에서도 두드러지게 나타난다. 어린이들은 자신의 마음 속 어휘사전에 아직 저장되

어 있지 않은 어휘들을 자신이 그동안 발견하고 나름대로 확립한 조어 규칙
에 따라 만들어서 그때그때 사용하기도 한다. 이러한 단어들은 한 언어공동
체의 사전 어휘를 유추함으로써 만들어진 것이며 해당언어의 '유사 조어 원
리'에 준거한 결과이다. 이러한 본래 의미의 일반 조어와는 근본적으로 차이
는 있지만 결과적으로 조어에 포함될 수 있는 현상이 바로 '관용구[1]에서 파생
되어 축소된 형태의 조어'이다. '어휘화된 복합적 언어단위 lexikalisierte
komplexe sprachliche Einheiten'라는 관용구의 정의에서 알 수 있듯이 관용
구는 일반적인 단순어나 복합어와 마찬가지로 한 언어의 어휘체계를 구성
하는 주요 언어단위이다. 자유로운 어휘들의 연결체가 이 형태로 오랜 기간
지속적인 사용을 통해 고정된 표현인 관용구는 형성 원리 측면에 있어서
조어 원리와 매우 유사하다. 즉, 기존의 어휘 체계에 존재하는 구성성분을
토대로 새로운 어휘가 생성된다는 점에서 출발하여 관용구와 조어는 의미
적, 구조적, 기능적 유사성을 지닌다.[2] 따라서 관용구에서 파생된 조어 역시
여타 일반 조어와 큰 공통점을 보인다. 그러나 전술한 공통점에도 불구하고
일반 조어와 '관용구에서 파생된 조어'는 근본적인 차이점을 보인다. 기존의
조어들이 대체로 두 개 이상의 형태소나 개별 어휘들이 서로 '결합'하여 '확
장'하는 과정 속에서 하나의 어휘 단위를 형성한다면, '관용구에서 파생된
조어'는 이미 두 개 이상의 어휘들로 이루어진 복합적 어휘체가 탈락을 통한

---

1   관용구 Phraseologismen는 Burger(2003:35)에 따르면 구조적, 의미적 그리고 화용적으
    로 매우 이질적이며 문장성분 단위에서 텍스트 단위에 이르는 광범위한 언어단위를 의
    미한다. 그 중에서 조어와 연관관계를 맺고 있는 부류는 "명명 관용구 nominative
    Phraseologismen"(Fleischer 1997:122, Burger 2003:37)이다. 따라서 본고의 주된 연구
    대상은 이러한 명명 관용구가 될 것이다.

2   Feilke(2004:59)는 관용구와 조어가 화용적으로 서로 상보적인 관계라고 말한다. 특히
    이러한 화용적 상보성은 말하기에서 서로 다른 역할을 하는 것으로 나타난다고 설명하
    고 있다.

'축소 결합 과정'을 거치면서 만들어지게 된다. 물론 이러한 축소과정의 동인으로는 언어 경제성의 원리가 작용한다.

이 논문에서는 언어변화의 관점에서 관용구와 관용구에서 파생된 조어와의 관계를 고찰하고 나아가 관용구를 압축 축소된 조어로 변화를 가능하게 하는 동인과 원리를 구체적인 실증적 자료를 통해 밝히고자 한다. 이를 위해 관용구의 기저 하에 파생된 독일어의 탈관용구화 조어를 수집하여 이를 유형에 따라 분류하여, 그 형성 동인에 대하여 다각도로 분석할 것이다.

2. 관용구

관용구는 한 언어시스템을 구성하는 언어단위 중에서 두 개 이상의 어휘로 구성된 언어표현으로, 이는 상대적 고정성을 띠는 다어휘결합체 Mehrworteinheit mit relativer Festigkeit이다.[3] 이러한 관용구의 형태통사적, 의사소통적 관점에 따라 다양한 하위영역으로 구분될 수 있다. 예를 들어 Burger(2003:33ff.)는 관용구를 기호학적 관점에 따라 지시적 referentiell, 구조적 strukurell, 의사소통적 kommunikativ 관용구로 분류하였다.[4] 관용구의 형식적(문장 성분가치, 문장 가치, 텍스트 가치), 의미적 숙어성 Idiomatizität의

---

3 관용구에 대한 정의에서 관용구 속성 자체도 그러하지만, 관용구 연구와 코퍼스언어학과의 접맥으로 관용구와 비관용구 언어단위 및 관용구의 하위분류가 뚜렷하게 구분하기 쉽지 않다. 실제 사용되는 언어자료의 분석은 관용구에 대한 정의 및 하위분류를 언어사용의 관점에서 기존 관용구론의 입장에서보다 상당히 유연하게 처리하면서 관용구의 특성 중에서 관습성을 강조하고 있다(Steyer 2013:21f.).

4 이외에도 관용구의 하위 범주화에 대해서는 Fleischer(1997, 99f./250f.), Korhonen/Wotjak (2001, 224f.) 등 참조.

정도를 복합적으로 고려하여 관용구의 하위부류를 시도하면, 일차적으로 문장 단위를 기준으로 '문장 하위 단위의 관용구'와 문장 상위의 단위로 기능하는 '문장 이상의 관용구'로 분류될 수 있다(Korhonen/Wotjak 2001:266). 문장 이상의 관용구에는 속담이나 상투적 문장과 상투적 텍스트 등이 포함되며 관용어휘소 Phraseolexeme, 연어 Kollokationen, (문장성분으로서) 상투어 (satzgliedwertige) Routineformeln, 기능동사구 Funktionsverbgefüge 등이 문장 아래 단위의 관용구에 해당된다.

관용구 중에서 관용어휘소 Phraseolexeme는 관용적 표현의 특징을 총체적으로 드러내고 있어 관용구의 핵심영역이라고 할 수 있다. 문장 성분으로 기능할 수 있는 다른 범주들과는 달리—예를 들어 연어, 기능동사구, 상투어—관용어휘소 혹은 관용어 Idiome는 항상 숙어성 Idiomatizität를 지니고 있다. 원래 숙어성은 초기 관용구 연구에서 관용구 개념을 규정하는 데에 있어서 가장 중요한 준거였으나, 관용구 연구의 발달과정 속에서 숙어성은 관용구 내에서 관용구를 하위분류하는 주요 기준점이 되었다(Stein 1995:35). 후기 관용구론 학자들은 숙어 성이 관용구와 다른 언어현상들을 구분하는 주요 척도가 아니라, 오히려 언어에 보편적이고 편재한다는 인식에 이르렀기 때문이다(Dobrovol'skij/Piirainen 1997:60).

숙어성은 관용 표현 자체가 지시하는 관용 의미 phraseologische Bedeutung와 관용 표현을 구성하는 개별 요소들의 의미들의 합에 해당하는 자유 의미 freie Bedeutung 혹은 축자적 의미 사이의 '의미의 비합성성'을 말한다 (Fleischer 1997:35; Burger et al. 1982:3). 'in die Pfanne hauen'과 같이 숙어성은 관용어의 구성요소들의 개별 의미들의 합과 해당 어휘결합체의 관용적 의미가 서로 전혀 관계가 없거나 혹은 'blinder Passagier'와 같이 구성요소들 간에 부분적 연관성이 있는 경우에 존재한다. 따라서 숙어성은 "언어 생산

성 규칙만으로는 전달되지 않는 지식에 대한 필요성"(Dobrovol'skij 1995:20)
에 대한 근거가 되기도 한다. 숙어성을 띠는 관용구의 축자적 의미는 대부분
진실조건을 고려한 현실 세계에서는 부조리하게 느껴지게 된다. 이런 경우
관용구는 하나의 구성구조 Konstrukt로서 이해할 수밖에 없다(Dobrovol'skij
1997:117).

관용구의 숙어성은 구성요소의 관용 의미와 관련 여부에 따라 총체적 숙
어성 Vollidiomatizität과 부분적 숙어성 Teilidiomatizität, 비숙어성으로 분
리될 수 있으며 이들 단계간의 경계는 유동적이다. 숙어성은 관용구의 축자
적 의미와 관용적 의미와의 관계에서 발생하므로 사실 의미의 유연성
Motiviertheit와 긴밀한 관계에 있다. 왜냐하면 유연성은 전체 관용구나 관용
구를 이루는 구성요소의 축자적 의미가 관용적 의미의 생성과 이해에 관여
하기 때문이다(Burger 2003:66f.). 은유적 관용구의 경우 구체적인 개념 영역
에서 추상적 영역으로의 전이에 대한 이해의 성공여부는 우선적으로 관용
구의 의미를 정확히 알 때에 가능하다는 점에서 유연성과 숙어성의 관계는
더욱 명확해진다.

관용구의 주요 특징인 고정성은 모든 언어 측면에서의 '절대적 확정성'을
의미하는 것이 아니라 점층적이고 상대적인 개념이다. 고정성 스펙트럼에는
모든 측면에서 고정된 어휘결합체가 한쪽 끝에 있다면 다른 한쪽 끝에는
상당히 느슨한 고정성을 지닌 관용구가 위치하게 된다. Burger(2003, 16ff.)는
고정성을 어휘 결합체의 통용성을 기준으로 심리언어적, 구조적, 화용적 측
면으로 구분하였다. 구조적 고정성은 형태 통사적 비규칙성 및 제약성과
어휘 의미적 제약에 의해 드러나게 되며 숙어성과 밀접한 관계를 지닌다.
고정성과 연관 관계 속에서 이해해야 할 또 다른 개념은 가변성 Variabilität
이다. 가변성은 관용구의 보편적 변이형이나 동의어나 임시적 변형에서 볼

수 있으며, 이는 관용구의 '상대적 고정성'에 대한 증거이기도 하다. 화용적 고정성은 특정 상황에 전형적으로 나타나는 관용구의 쓰임새를 말하는 것으로 이런 화용적 고정성이 대표적으로 드러나는 것은 무엇보다도 상투구이다.

고정성은 다른 한편으로는 반복성 Wiederholung을 의미한다. 관용구의 반복성은 일련의 발화연속체로서 특정 덩어리가 계속 반속해서 사용되어 인간의 기억에 각인되어 저장되는 과정을 반영하고 있다. 이는 결국 재생성 Reproduduzierbarkeit를 의미한다. 즉, 관용구는 의사소통에서 자유선택 원칙에 의해서 구와 문장을 매번 새로 생성하는 것이 아니라, '이미 조립된 ready made' 조각들의 결합체를 그대로 재생하여 문장이 만들어 지는 것이다. Fleischer(1997:63)는 원칙적으로는 관용구의 특징으로 재생성에 반대하는 입장을 견지하지만 적어도 관용구 사용에 있어서는 재생산성이 결정적인 기준이 될 수 있다고는 인정하였다.

3. 탈관용구화 조어

탈관용구화 조어 dephraseologische Wortbildungskonstruktionen는 관용구를 기반으로 언어경제성에 기반하여 생성된 복합어다. Fleischer(1997:185ff.)는 관용구의 기저 하에 생성된 이러한 언어현상을 "탈관용구화 파생어 dephraseologische Derivation"로 명명하였다. 이 탈관용구화 파생어에는 명시적인 파생과정의 결과물뿐만 아니라 내포적 파생어와 다른 유형의 조어들도 포함되어 있다. 따라서 Fleischer(1997:185ff.)에 의해 명명된 '탈관용구화 파생어'는 아주 폭넓은 의미로 이해되어야 한다. 탈관용구화 조어의 예를 살펴보자.

(1) jm. Honig an die Backe/um den Bart/um den Mund/um das Maul
    schmieren → der Honig

(2) sich wichtig tun → der Wchtigtuer

(3) einen krummen Buckel machen → der Krummbuckel

위의 (1)~(3)에서 볼 수 있듯이, Fleischer가 명명한 '탈관용구화 파생어'
에는 파생어의 일반적 특징인 비자립적 형태소가 포함되어 있는 경우도 있
고 그렇지 않은 경우도 있다. 탈관용구화 파생어는 관용구를 구성하는 특정
요소에 의한 대치, 특정요소에 접사를 추가한 파생, 특정요소들로의 합성
등의 다양한 구조적 형태를 띠고 있다. 따라서 이러한 연구 대상을 모두
포괄할 수 있는 새로운 용어가 필요하다는 인식하에 본고에서는 '탈관용구
화 조어'라는 용어를 선택하였다. 탈관용구화 조어는 기존의 탈관용구화 파
생어라는 개념이 갖고 있는 관념적 제약을 극복할 수 있는 적절한 개념이라
고 할 수 있다.

기저 관용구의 관용적 의미와 그 조어의 의미와의 연관성은 탈관용구화
조어에서 중요한 부분이다. 기저 관용구와 그에 대응하는 조어는 의미적으
로 서로 연관성을 지니며 서로 동일한 대상을 지시하거나 적어도 의미의
핵은 일치한다.[5] 예를 들어 steif wie Stock → stocksteif나 schwarzer Markt

---

5 어휘 구조적으로 서로 연관성이 있을 것으로 보이는 관용구와 조어가 의미적으로 아무
   런 관련이 없는 경우는 ein stilles Wasser와 Stillwasser, alte Meister와 Altmeister 등이
   있다. 이러한 예들은 탈관용구화 조어라고 할 수 없으므로 본고에서는 다루지 않을 것
   이다.

→ Schwarzmarkt는 관용구의 의미와 핵심 구성요소와 그에서 비롯된 조어의 의미 및 구성요소가 서로 거의 일치하는 경우이고 jm. einen Korb geben → der Korb의 경우에서는 관용구의 관용적 의미 중에서 핵심적 의미를 지니고 있는 구성요소 Korb만이 탈관용구화 조어의 표층구조에 나타나고 있다.

[그림 1] 기저관용구의 탈관용구화 조어 과정

[그림 1]에서 볼 수 있듯이 기저 관용구는 탈락 혹은 축소 그리고 결합과 첨가라는 언어처리과정을 거쳐 관용구의 기저 구조를 버리고 조어 구조를 띠게 된다. 이러한 처리 과정이 개개의 어휘생성에 모두 나타나는 것은 아니다. 기저 관용구에서 조어로의 언어처리 방향은 비교적 생산성이 높은 반면, 그에 대한 가역과정, 즉 일반 조어가 관용구로 확대되는 과정은 매우 드물다고 할 수 있다. pechschwarz, spindeldürr, nudeldick과 같은 조어는 원래는 이에 기저하고 있는 관용구가 존재하지 않은 예이지만(Fleischer 1997:339), 실제 언어사용에서 schwarz wie Pech와 같은 비유 관용구를 발견할 수 있음을 볼 때 조어에서 관용구로 전이된 경우라고도 말할 수 있을 것이다.[6]

---

6 모든 비유 관용구가 합성어로 전이되는 것은 아니다. 예를 들어 stolz wie Spanier나 gesund wie ein Fisch와 같은 예에서는 *spanierstolz나 *fischgesund와 같은 조어는 형성될 수 없다. 따라서 비유 관용구에서 조어로의 전이가 가능한 경우들의 특징에 대한 연구도 매우 흥미로운 관점이다.

탈관용구화 조어는 행위자, 행위성, 행위의 결과, 소유관계 등 다양한 의미적 관계를 나타낼 수 있다. 독일어에서는 탈동사화된 탈관용구화 명사가 가장 생산성이 높으며 그에 따라 의미적 관계의 측면에서도 행위자나 행위성 등의 조어 명사가 우세하게 나타난다(Fleischer 1997:186).

[표 1] 탈관용구화 조어의 의미관계

기저 관용구	처리 과정		탈관용구화 조어	의미관계
Possen reißen	탈락		Possenreißer	Nomen agentis
Bericht erstatten	첨가	⟹	Berichterstattung	Nomen actionis
In Kraft treten	결합		Inkrafttreten	Nomen acti

위의 [표 1]에서 볼 수 있듯이 관용구 구성요소들이 결합한 후 -er, -ung, -(er)ei, -e, 무접사 등의 조어 접미사가 첨가되면서—경우에 따라서는 첨가 현상이 먼저 일어난 후 결합이 되기도 한다—탈관용구화 조어의 다양한 의미관계가 형성된다. 특히, 관용구 중에서 숙어성 Idiomatizität이 거의 없다고 할 수 있는 기능 동사구의 탈관용구화의 조어형성을 자주 볼 수 있으며, 이 경우에는 행위성 Nomen actionis이나 행위 결과 Nomen acti의 의미관계가 주로 나타난다.

독일어의 경우 탈관용구화 조어의 기저로는 동사 관용구의 빈도수가 높은데, 이는 독일어 관용구 자체의 범주적 분포의 편향성에 기인한다고 볼 수 있다. 즉, 독일어에서는 동사 관용구가 명사 관용구나 형용사 관용구에 비하여 매우 발달되어 있기 때문이다.[7]

---

7   Fleischer(1996:336)에 의하면 독일어에서는 조어의 경우 명사 조어가 우세한 반면 관용

탈관용구화 조어와 일정 정도 유사하지만 본질적으로 구분되는 언어 현상은 "관용구의 파생어 phraseologische Derivation"(Fleischer 1997:189)이다. 관용구 파생어는 관용구 목록의 다양화 과정으로서 변이형에 의해 만들어진다. 관용구 변이형이 구성요소의 형태 통사적 측면의 부분적 변형에 머무르지 않고 관용구 구성어휘 자체가 바뀔 때에 관용구 파생어가 생성된다.

> (4) in der Klemme/Patsche/Tinte sitzen

> (5) unter die Räder/den Schlitten kommen

(4)~(5)의 예에서 볼 수 있듯이 관용구적 파생어는 구성요소의 대체를 통해 결국 관용적 동의어 phraseologische Synonyme를 형성한다. 따라서 관용구적 파생어는 의미적으로 관용구 상호 간에 동의 관계에 놓여 있다. 관용구 파생어에 있어서 기저 관용구와 파생 관용구의 구분은 어휘의 통사적 고찰에 의해 가능하다.

4. 탈관용구화 조어로의 변형 유형

관용구를 기저로 생성된 탈관용구화 조어는 형성원리에 있어서 다양한 양상을 보인다. 우선 양적인 측면에서 살펴보면 관용구를 이루고 있는 특정 개별 어휘 하나가 탈관용구화 조어가 되는 경우에서부터 관용구 구성요소

구에 있어서는 동사 관용구의 비중이 크다고 한다. 이러한 양적 분포는 언어마다 서로 상이하다.

전체가 새로운 어휘 형성에 관여하는 경우도 있다.

   (6) Garn spinnen → das Garn

   (7) jm. Löcher in den Bauch/Leib fragen → löchern

   (8) einen blauen Montag machen → blaumachen

   (9) Gott verdamm mich → gottverdammmich

예제 (6)과 (7)은 관용구의 단일 구성요소의 탈관용구화 조어를 보여주는 예로 각각 관용구를 이루고 있는 명사나 동사 구성요소만이 탈관용구화 조어로 남게된 경우이다. (9)는 관용구 구성요소 전체가 조어 형성에 참여하는 경우이다. 그리고 관용구를 구성하는 어휘 요소 중에서 두 개의 관용구 구성요소만이 새로운 조어에 남아서 기저 관용구의 대신하고 나머지 구성요소는 생략되는 경우가 (8)이다. (8)의 경우를 자세히 살펴보면, 그 구성요소 중에서 관용구의 의미의 핵을 담당하고 있는 어휘는 blau와 Montag 그리고 의미치에 있어서 일정정도 비어 있다고 할 수 있는 machen이다. 이 중에서 blau와 machen이 새로운 조어에 관여하고 있다. 이는 탈관용구화 조어 연구에 있어서 고려해야 할 중요한 관점이다. 즉 구체적으로 기저 관용구의 구성요소 중에 어떤 구성요소, 그리고 몇 개의 구성요소가 조어형성에 관여하여 새로운 조어를 구성하는가 문제와 그리고 이 경우 새로운 조어를 만드는 원리와 형성동인은 무엇인가에 관한 문제는 관용구화 조어연구의 주요 논의의 대상이 된다.

   탈관용구화 조어의 유형분류에 있어서 우선 관용구를 대표하는 단일어 의미 유형이 있다. 단일어 의미 유형은 한 개의 관용구 구성요소를 제외하고 나머지 모든 요소가 탈락되는 경우로, 전체 관용구를 대표하게 되는 어휘는 관용적 의미를 그대로 흡수하거나 혹은 관용적 의미의 핵만을 전이 받아 의미적으로 독립하게 된다(Häcki-Buhofer 2002:135). 탈관용구화 조어를 생성하는 관용구의 이러한 구성요소는 일반적 커뮤니케이션에 그 하나의 단어만으로도 충분히 전체 관용구를 연상할 수 있게 해주는 어휘이다.

(10) jm. Honig an die Backe/um den Bart/um den Mund/um das Maul schmieren → der Honig: Ausgeheckt hat sie der Chef der Stadtwerke, Peter Heister. Und mit Oberbürgermeister Andreas Michelmann (Widab) hat er schon einen prominenten Befürworter an Land gezogen. „Wir können nicht nur in Sonntagsreden der Jugend *Honig ums Maul schmieren*, wir müssen den Jugendlichen auch was bieten", so Michelmann. Deshalb habe er sich für Heisters Idee schnell erwärmen können. (https://www.mz.de/lokal/aschersleben/jugendarbeit-in-aschersleben-nicht-nur-honig-ums-maul-schmieren-14238 96, 2022.2.10. 검색)

(11) jm. Dampf machen → der Dampf: Wir wollen *der Politik Dampf machen*. Der zweite Vorsitzende der IG Metall, Detlef Wetzel, hat die Parteien aufgefordert, „Politik für die Mehrheit der Menschen" zu machen. Eine Mitgliederumfrage habe ergeben, dass sich eine große Mehrheit eine „gerechtere Gesellschaft" wünsche. (https://www.deutschlandfunk.de/wetzel-wir-wollen-der-politik-dampf-machen-100.html, 2022.2.10. 검색)

위의 예들은 기저 관용구의 구성요소 중에서 하나의 명사가 그대로 탈관용구화 조어가 된 경우이다. 예 (10)의 Honig는 기저 관용구의 관용적 의미인 '진실되지 않은 말을 하다' 혹은 '아부하다'를 조어에서 그대로 전이 받게 되어 독자적인 의미를 획득한 것이다. (11)의 Dampf도 마찬가지로 기저 관용구의 의미인 '독려하다', '다그치다'에서 출발하여 '극한 노력'라는 의미로 관용구 외적으로 독자적 쓰임이 가능한 어휘로 기능한다. 이와 같이 다어휘 단위의 의미가 압축 축소된 어휘로 대체로 소급되어 전이되는 처리 과정을 Fleischer(1997:142)는 관용구 구성요소의 의미적 독립이라는 관점에서 '자립화 Autonomisierung'라고 명명하였다. 이제 관용구의 의미를 대변하는 다른 품사들도 살펴보자.

> (12) den Rahm abschöpfen → abschpöfen: Landwirte wettern gegen Preisverfall: Selbst *den Rahm abschöpfen*. Ständig neue Gesetze: Das macht Landwirten oft mehr zu schaffen als Unkraut oder Hagel. Der Bayerische Bauernverband (BBV) will da Sprachrohr sein, doch nicht überall finden sich Obmänner, um vor Ort als Mittler zu fungieren. (https://www.onetz.de/thanstein/vermischtes/landwirte-wettern-gegen-pre isverfall-selbst-den-rahm-abschoepfen-d1708206.html, 2022.2.10. 검색)
>
> (13) die Suppe auslöfffeln, die man sich eingebrockt hat → einbrocken: Dubé muss die Suppe auslöffeln, die er sich eingebrockt hat. Gottéron in Not. Die Drachen drohen nach zwei Pleiten, den Kontakt zu den Playoff-Plätzen verlieren. (https://www.blick.ch/sport/eishockey/nla/luft-wird-fuer-fribourg-duenn-dube-muss-die-suppe-ausloeffeln-die-er-sich-eingebrockt-hat-id15710669.html, 2022.2.10. 검색)

(12)~(13)에서는 관용구를 구성하고 있는 동사가 관용구 전체의 의미를 전이 받고 있다. 사실 관용구 전체를 대표하여 독립적 기능을 할 수 있는

관용구 구성요소는 일반적으로 그 관용구에서 통사적으로 지배적인 품사들인 경우가 대부분이다. 이러한 어휘는 관용구의 핵어 Kennwort에 해당되기도 한다. 예를 들어 동사 관용구에서는 그 관용구를 구성하고 있는 동사, 형용사 관용구에서는 형용사, 명사 관용구에서는 명사가 관용구 외적 자립 어휘로 쓰이면서 관용적 의미를 전수 받을 잠재적 가능성을 지니고 있다.

(14) bei jm. ins Fettnäpfen treten → Fettnäpfen: Das 3. Soloprogramm von Florian Rexer 2020/21 zeigt REXER, wie er täglich als gebürtiger Deutscher in neue Schweizer-*Fettnäpfchen* tappt. (https://rexer.ch/comedy/fettnaepfchen/ 2022.2.10. 검색)

(15) Kohldampf schieben → Kohldampf: Das perfekte *Kohldampf?* – aus der Tajine, und trotzdem ganz bodenständig-Rezept mit Bild und einfacher Schritt-für-Schritt-Anleitung.(https://www.kochbar.de 2022.2.10. 검색)

(16) auf dem Holzweg sein → Holzweg: Der Begriff „*Holzweg*" steht für einen Weg, der in einem Wald angelegt wurde, um Holz zu beschaffen, und nicht der Verbindung zweier Orte dient, also nicht zum Ziel führt. Wie Sie Holzwege in der Führung erkennen und was Sie machen, wenn Sie doch auf dem Holzweg sind, erfahren Sie hier. (https://juergenwulff.de/orientierungszeit-podcast-038/ 2022.2.10. 검색)

(14)~(15)는 사실 동사들이 관용구의 핵심어이기는 하지만 관용적 의미를 전이 받아 독립성을 획득한 어휘는 명사 합성어 Fettnäpfen과 Kohldampf이다. 예 (16)은 계사 sein으로 인해 동사관용구 여부에 대해 논란의 여지가 있지만 Holzweg이 독립적으로 쓰일 수 있는 어휘이다.[8]

탈관용구 조어의 두 번째 유형은 파생어이다. 파생어는 관용구의 한 어휘나 핵심구성요소에 접사가 첨가되는 경우이다. 이 파생어 역시 기저 관용구의 관용적 의미를 그대로 혹은 부분적으로 전이 받아 유지하고 있다.

(17) sich jn./etw. auf den Hals laden → aufhalsen

(18) jm. Wurst/Wurscht sein → wurstig

예 (17)은 관용구의 구성요소 Hals에서 파생된 동사 aufhalsen에 기저 관용구의 관용적 의미가 흡수되어 있는 경우이며 (18)의 경우에는 명사 Wurst의 형용사형에 관용적 의미가 전이되어 있다.

탈관용구화 조어의 세 번째 유형은 합성어이다. 이 유형의 특징은 탈관용화 조어를 이루는 요소들이 특정한 결합을 위한 언어적 수단 없이 어휘들이 결합하여 구성된다는 점이다. 이때 관용구를 이루는 구성요소들에 붙어있는 문법적 형태소들은 탈락하지만, 그 외의 어떤 조어 형태소의 추가 없이 새로운 합성어가 생성된다.

(19) einen krummen Buckel machen → der Krummbuckel

(20) blau wie ein Veilchen → das Blauveilchen

관용구를 기저로 하여 생성되는 합성어는 빈도 높은 탈관용구화 조어 중의 하나이다. 특히, '~wie~'라는 형식의 '비유 관용구 Komparative Phraseologismen'

---

8   관용구의 구성요소로서의 계사 sein에 대하여 Fleischer(1996:337)는 형용사가 들어 있는 비유 관용구의 경우에 있어서는 sein을 필수적 구성요소로 간주하여 동사관용구에 포함시켰다.

는 이러한 탈관용구화 합성어의 주요 원천이라고 할 수 있는데, 이때 관용구의 형용사 구성요소가 기본어휘가 되며 명사구성요소는 한정적 역할을 하게 된다.

(21) dünn/ fein wie ein Haar → haardünn

(22) grob wie ein Sack → sackgrob

(23) stark wie ein Bär → bärenstark

명사나 형용사 합성어 이외에도 동사 합성어도 찾아 볼 수 있다. 예를 들면 다음과 같다.

(24) jn. an der Nase herum führen → nasführen

탈관용구화 조어 원리에 있어서 위에서 언급한 파생과 합성이 동시에 일어나는 경우도 있다.

(25) einen Riss/ Risse im Hirn haben → hirnrissig

(26) Grillen fangen → der Grillenfänger

(27) jm. ins Auge/ in die Augen fallen → augenfällig

위의 (25)~(27)는 합성과 파생이 동시에 일어난 경우이다. (23)은 Hirn과 Riss의 결합형에 형용사 접미사 -ig가 첨가되어 생성된 것이며 (24)~(25)는 파생과 합성의 조어 과정이 순차적으로 일어난 경우이다.

네 번째 탈관용구화 조어는 축약어 Kurzwortbildung이다. 탈관용구화 축약어는 관용구의 구성요소들이 대부분 탈락되며 이때 탈관용구화 조어를 이루는 부분은 관용구 구성요소들의 두음 철자들이다. 이 점에서 단일어휘에 의한 탈관용구화 조어 형성과의 차이점을 보인다.

    (28) j(g)anz weit draußen → jwd

jwd는 j(g)anz weit draußen의 두음으로 구성되어 이루어진 어휘로서 일상어에서 농담조로 사용된다. 이 조어는 실제 독일어의 어휘를 생성하는 음운규칙에도 맞지 않은 조합이다. 이러한 축약어는 사실 매우 드문 현상이다.

5. 탈관용화 조어의 동인

지금까지는 독일어 탈관용구화 조어의 정의 및 특징과 그 유형을 살펴보았다. 이 장에서는 이러한 조어 형성이 발생하게 된 동인을 언어적 동기화의 관점에서 살펴보고자 한다.

언어기호에서 시니피에와 시니피앙 사이의 관계는 필연적이 것이 아니라 자의적이며, 이러한 자의성은 언어의 본질적 특징이다. 그러나 단순어가 아닌 합성어나 비숙어적 관용구와 숙어적 관용구는 그 언어기호를 구성하고 있는 요소에 의해 상당히 동기화된 경우가 많이 있다. 그러므로 인지언어학자들은 오히려 언어가 기본적으로 동기화되어 있는 것으로 보고 있다.[9]

---

9   소쉬르는 언어 기호의 자의성을 언어의 본질적 특징으로 간주하면서도 어휘의 유형에 따라 동기화에 대해서도 언급하였다(Saussure 1967:79ff.). 그러나 소쉬르와 인지 언어학 입장의 동기화에 대한 입장은 근본적으로 상이하다. 소쉬르는 자의성이 기본적인 것

Lakoff/Johnson(1999:464)은 대부분의 언어가 전적으로 자의적인 것도 아니며 전적으로 예측 가능한 것도 아니라 오히려 어느 정도 동기화되어 있다고 하였으며 Radden/Panther(2004:2)은 이러한 동기화가 자의성과 예측가능성의 양극단 사이에 있는 연속적 영역으로 보았다.

　동기화는 언어의 형태와 내용이 자의적인 관계에 놓여 있는 것이 아니라 서로 연관성이 있음을 의미한다. 즉, 언어의 내용과 형태가 언어 독립적 요소에 의해 영향을 받아 형성됨을 의미한다. 언어의 내용과 형태에 영향을 미치는 언어 독립적 요인으로는 세상에 대한 경험, 지각적 현저성 원리, 의사소통의 경제성 등이 있다. 이러한 언어 독립적 요소를 그림으로 나타내면 다음과 같다.

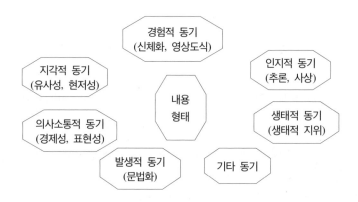

[그림 2] 언어 독립적 동기화 요인(Radden/Panther 2004:24)

　이며 동기화는 자의성의 제한으로 간주하지만 인지언어학에서는 그와는 반대로 동기화가 근본적이며 자의성은 마지막 수단으로 여기는 입장이다.

위 [그림 2]의 동기화에 대해 간략하게 살펴보면 경험의 동기화는 신체를 통한 경험에 의해 발생하는 영상도식이 언어에 동기를 부여하는 것이며, 지각적 동기화는 주의, 유사성, 관점 조절 등이 언어 동기부여 기제이다. 예를 들어 한국어의 나사돌리개와 독일어의 Schraubenzieher의 경우 동일한 대상의 명명에 있어서 한국어에서는 돌리는 동작에 집중되는 반면 독일어의 경우는 당겨서 빼는 동작에 주의기 집중된다. 의사소통적 동기화의 경우는 경제성과 명시성을 기반으로 하는 의사소통 활동에서 비롯된 것이다. 특이 줄임말이나 혼성어 등이 이에 해당하는 대표적인 사례이다. 발생적 동기화는 과거의 언어형태가 현재 다른 기능이나 형태로 작용하는 동기로 문법화 현상이 이에 해당된다. 인지적 동기화는 인간이 지식구조에 접근하는 능력과 관련된 동기이다. 이러한 동기화 요인들은 서로 교차 작용할 수 있으며 인간이 세계를 인식하는 방식을 드러내주는 것이다.

탈관용구화 조어과정를 야기하는 동인은 다양하다. 관용구의 의미가 그 구성요소들의 의미의 합은 아니지만 그 의미가 어느 정도는 그 구성요소의 어떤 특정 국면과 관련된 경우가 많이 있으므로 관용구는 동기화되어 있는 언어기호 중의 하나라고 할 수 있다.[10] 관용구와 같은 복합적인 표현을 선택과 축약 및 결합 등의 처리를 통해 새로운 어휘를 형성하는 데에는 어떤 개념의 망이나 인지모형이 작용하게 된다고 볼 수 있는데, 이 때 선택의 동인으로 경제성과 현저성 그리고 환유와 같은 요소가 작용할 수 있다.

탈관용구화 조어를 야기하는 동인에 대해 구체적으로 살펴보면, 여러 개

---

10 Lakoff(1987:147)는 합성어 의미의 예측 불가능성에 대하여 언급하였고 Langacker(2000: 16)는 복잡한 표현의 의미가 구성요소의 특정 측면과의 연관되어 있으며 따라서 동기화 되어 있음을 주장하였다. 이러한 주장은 합성어와 형성 원리와 과정이 유사한 관용구에 도 해당된다.

의 구성요소로 이루어진 관용구를 복합어로 만든다는 점에 있어서 탈관용
구화 조어에는 인간 행동이나 심리의 보편적 특성인 최소의 노력으로 최대
의 효과를 거두려는 경제성의 원리, 즉 의사소통적 동기화가 작동한다. 사실
탈관용구화 조어의 근간을 이루고 있는 동인은 언어경제성이라고도 할 수
있다. 이때, 경제성은 생략, 축소 등의 언어 단순화 현상으로 나타난다.

(29) schlafen wie ein Dachs → dachsen

(30) jm. ein paar hinter die Löffel geben → löffeln

위 (29)~(30)의 예는 관용구에서 파생된 조어가 기존 관용적 표현보다
감정 가치면에서 더 강한 효과를 주는 경우이다(Fleischer 1997:188). 단순 어
휘와 관용구를 구분해 주는 관용구의 주요 특징 중의 하나가 '표현적 가치증
대 expressiver Mehrwert'지만, 이러한 표현성의 증대라는 특이성이 탈관용
구화 조어에서 더 두드러지게 나타날 수도 있다. 이러한 감정가치의 증대라
는 언중의 욕구가 탈관용구화 조어의 형성에 기여하게 된다. 이것 또한 의사
소통적 동기화, 즉 표현성에 대한 동인으로 작용한다. 경제성의 또 다른 측
면은 어휘 저장을 위한 간략화이다. 두 개 이상의 어휘로 구성되는 관용구를
마음 사전에 그대로 저장하기에는 부담스러운 것일 수 있다. 구성요소의
양을 저장에 용이한 단위로 축소하려는 성향 역시 탈관용구의 조어화의 원
동력이기도 하다.

(31) dünne Bretter bohren/ das Brett bohren, wo es am dünnsten ist → der
Dünnbrettbohrer

(32) auf Lauer liegen → auflauern

언어사용자가 조어를 만들 때에는 특정 대상에 이름을 붙이기 위한 기초로서 제공되는 복잡한 근원(ICM)이 있다. 현저성이나 환유와 같은 언어 독립적 요인을 통해 복잡한 근원 내에 있는 특정 구성요소가 언어공동체에 의해 선택되어 조어가 형성된다. 이때 선택된 부분은 전체를 대신하며 현저한 부분이 전체 근원을 효율적으로 떠오르게 만든다. 탈관용구화 조어에서도 전체 관용구를 가장 효율적으로 떠오르게 할 수 있는 대표성을 띠는 어휘나 구성요소가 조어가 관여하게 되고 나머지 요소는 생략된다.

(33) den Rahm abschöpfen → abschöpfen
(34) einen blauen Montag machen → blaumachen

위의 예 중에서 (33)는 현저성에 의한 선택의 경우로 Rahm과 abschöpfen 두 구성요소 중에 좋은 부분 그 자체를 나타내는 어휘보다 그 부분을 골라서 떠내는 행동을 나타내는 동사가 관용구를 대신하는 어휘로 선택되어 관용적 의미를 전이받고 있다.

기존의 표현, 특히 문체 체계에서 낮은 층위의 관용구들을 완곡하게 표현하거나 일상 커뮤니케이션의 규범에 일정정도 부합되게 미화하려는 욕구가 탈관용구화의 동기가 되기도 한다. 현대 독일어에서 문체상 낮은 관용구들은 축약어의 형태로 은폐성을 띤 채로 쓰이기도 한다.

(35) Leck mich am Arsch! → LmA

6. 결론

본고에서는 독일어 조어와 그 생성 근간으로서 관용구와의 상호관계를 살펴보면서 관용구를 조어로 만들어 주는 동인에 대하여 논의하였다. 탈관용구화 조어는 관용구를 토대로 형성된 복합어이다. 다어휘성을 지닌 관용구와 조어는 사실 그 자체로도 서로 매우 밀접한 연관성을 지니고 있다. 이러한 연관성은 탈관용구화 조어에 일반 조어와 마찬가지로 파생어, 합성어, 축약어 등의 조어원리가 그대로 적용되고 있다는 사실에서도 나타난다. 의미적으로도 기저 관용구와 그에 대응하는 탈관용구화 조어는 서로 연관성을 지닌다. 즉, 탈관용구화 조어와 그 기저가 되는 관용구는 서로 동일한 대상을 지시하거나 적어도 의미의 핵심은 일치해야 하며 그렇지 않은 경우는 탈관용구화 조어라고 할 수 없다.

탈관용구화 조어의 동인은 동기화 이론에 근거하여 설명할 수 있다. 관용구의 의미가 어느 정도 그 구성요소의 어떤 특정 국면에 의해 좌우되므로 관용구 자체는 일정 정도 동기화된 언어기호 중의 하나라고 볼 수 있다. 복합적인 표현체를 특정 조작 원리를 통해 새로운 어휘를 형성하는 데에는 어떤 개념의 망이나 인지모형이 작용하게 된다. 이 경우 특정 구성요소를 선택하게 되는 동인은 경제성과 현저성과 같은 언어외적 요인이 결정적인 역할을 하게 된다. 탈관용구화 조어가 생성되는 데에는 근본적으로 경제성 원리가 작용하고 있다는 점은 논란의 여지가 없다. 그 외에 현저성이나 표현성 등의 원리도 탈관용구화 조어 형성의 주요 동인이라고 할 수 있다.

관용구와 그에 상응하는 탈관용구화 조어가 텍스트에서 실제로 어떻게 쓰이고 있으며, 각각의 실질적 사용에서 차이점이 존재하는지 여부와 관용구와 그에서 비롯된 조어 사이의 사용에 있어서 빈도 차이는 존재하는지 등에 관한 문제는 본고에서는 상세하게 다루지는 않았다. 이러한 문제에 대해서는 향후에 본 연구와의 연계 속에서 수행되어야 할 가치 있는 후속 연구 과제가 될 것이다.

참고문헌

정수정(2019), 관용구의 이해, 커뮤니케이션북스.

Barz. I. (2007), "Wortbildung und Phraseologie," In: Burger, H/ Dobrovol'skij, D./ Kühn, P./Norrick, N.-R.(Hrsg.): *Phraseologie, ein internationales Handbuch der zeitgenössischen Forschung*, Berlin/New York.

Burger, H. (2003), *Phraseologie. Eine Einführung am Beispiel des Deutschen*, Berlin.

Burger, H./Buhofer, A./ Sialm, A. (1982), *Handbuch der Phraseologie*. Berlin.

Dobrovol'skij, D. (1995), *Kognitive Aspekte der Idiom-Semantik. Studien zum Thesaurus deutscher Idiome*. Tübingen: Narr.

Dobrovol'skij, D. (1997), *Idiome im mentalen Lexikon*. Trier. Wissenschaftlicher Verlag.

Dobrovol'skij, D./Piirainen E. (1997), *Symbole in Sprache und Kultur -Studien zur Phraseologie aus kultursemiotischer Sicht*. Bochum.

Feilke, H. (2004), "Kontext-Zeichen-Kompentenz," In: Steyer, K. (Hg.), *Wortverbindungen - mehr oder weniger fest*, Berlin.

Fleischer, W. (1996), "Zum Verhältnis von Wortbildung und Phraseologie im Deutschen," In: Korhonen, J. (Hg.): *Studien zur Phraseologie des Deutschen und des Finnischen II*: Bochum.

Fleischer, W. (1997), *Phraseologie der deutschen Gegenwartssprache*, Tübingen.

Fleischer, W./Barz. I. (1995), *Wortbildung der deutschen Gegenwartssprache*, Tübingen.

Häcki-Buhofer, A. (2002), "Unikalia im Sprachwandel: phraseologisch gebundene Wörter und ihre lexikographische Erfassung," In: Piirainen, E./ Piirainen, I. T., (Hg.), *Phraseologie in Raum und Zeit, Baltmannsweiler*, 125-60.

Korhonen, J./Wotjak, B.(2001), "Kontrastivität in der Phraseologie," In: Helbig, Gerhard et al.(Hrsg.): *Deutsch als Fremdsprache. Ein internationales Handbuch*. Berlin, New York, 224-235.

Lakoff, G./Johnson, M. (1999), *Philosophy in the flesh: the embodied mind and its challenge to Western thought*, New York.

Langaker, R. (2000), *Grammar and conceptualization*, Berlin/New York.

Radden, G./Panther, K.‒U. (2004), "Introduction: Reflections on motivation," In: Radden, G./Panther, K.‒U. (ed.), *Studies in Linguistic Motivation*. Berlin/New York: Mouton de Gruyter.

Saussure, F. (2001), *Grundfragen der allgemeinen Sprachwissenschaft*, Lommel, H. (übers), Berlin: De Gruyter.

Stein, St. (1995), *Formelhafte Sprache. Untersuchungen zu ihren pragmatischen und kognitiven Funktionen im gegenwärtigen Deutsch*. Frankfurt/M.

Steyer, K. (2013), "Usuelle Wortverbindungen ‒ Zentrale Muster des Sprachgebrauchs aus korpusanalytischer Sicht". In: *Studien zur Deutschen Sprache 65*, Tübingen.

An Agree-Based Approach to Scrambling

Kwang-sup Kim

1. Introduction

Scrambling is mysterious in many respects. First of all, it is unclear why scrambling takes place. If movement is feature-driven, there must be a feature that is responsible for scrambling. However, it is hard to say which feature is responsible for it. Focus can be a candidate, but it is not the case that every scrambled phrase is focused. Second, if scrambling is a movement, we run into so-called scrambling paradoxes. Movement gives rise to scope effects, but scrambling over a scrambled phrase does not. If the relative word order between A and B is maintained, the scope relation between them is not changed even after multiple scrambling. This is puzzling under the movement approach to scrambling. With an eye into resolving these problems, this paper explores the possibility of providing a base-generation approach to scrambling.

Numerous linguists(e.g. Bošković 1994, Lasnik 1995, Bošković and Takahashi

1998, Hornstein 1999, 2001, Boeckx, Hornstein, and Nunes 2010) have proposed that thematic roles are features.[1] While assuming that they are correct, this article attempts to provide an AGREE-based account of thematic role assignment: i.e., I propose that thematic role assignment, just like Case assignment, takes place via the operation 'AGREE'. The AGREE theory comprises two major components: Probe and Goal(Chomsky 2000, 2001, 2008). Accordingly, the question naturally arises as to what functions as a probe and what as a goal in thematic role assignment. There are two possibilities: the thematic role of a predicate is a probe taking an argument as its goal, or an argument is a probe taking a thematic role as its goal. This article explores the second possibility while assuming that Chomsky's (1986) Visibility Condition is on the right track. According to the Visibility Condition, a link of a Case-marked chain is visible for theta-marking.

(1) Visibility Condition (Chomsky 1986)

A position in a Case-marked CHAIN is visible for theta-marking.

It is usually known that if an argument is assigned a thematic role, it can be assigned Case. According to the Visibility Condition in (1), however, the DP with Case can be assigned a thematic role.[2] To reinterpret the

---

1   On the other hand, Hale and Keyser(1993, 2002) and Chomsky(1995) propose that thematic roles are not features and hence thematic role assignment is not a feature-checking operation.

2   It is controversial as to whether Korean is a DP language or an NP language. I

Visibility from the perspective of Chomsky's(2001) Probe–Goal Theory, Case is a probe taking a thematic role as its goal.

(2) Revised Visibility Condition[3]

Case is a probe and its goal is a thematic role.

The essence of the Revised Visibility Condition is that the argument with Case requires a thematic role, not vice versa. If the Case of an argument is a probe and its goal is a thematic role, the argument may not be base–generated as the sister of the predicate.[4] The major goal of this article is to investigate the consequences of the Revised Visibility Condition. In this article I claim that the Revised Visibility Condition sheds light on various puzzles concerning scrambling, including scrambling paradoxes.

2. Scrambling Paradoxes

Japanese and Korean are strict head–final languages: that is, the head must occur in the final position. However, the order of the non–heads is relatively free, although the basic word order is SOV. Sentence (3b), for

---

tentatively assume that nominal arguments are DPs in Korean.

3   More precisely, the label of the DP with Case is a probe for a thematic role.

4   If the thematic role of a predicate is a probe and its goal is an argument, the argument must be the sister of the predicate, since the probe must c–command its goal.

instance, is perfectly grammatical as well as its unmarked counterpart (3a). The widely held view about this phenomenon, which is called scrambling, is that there is a relation between (3a) and (3b), and their relation can be captured by movement.

(3) a. Dareka-ga   daremo-o   aisite-iru. (Japanese)

someone-Nom   everyone-Acc   loves

'Someone loves everyone.' (someone>everyone; *everyone>someone)

b. Daremo-o   dareka-ga   aisite-iru.

everyone-Acc   someone-Nom   loves

'Someone loves everyone.' (someone>everyone; everyone>someone)

The movement approach seems to deal with the scope effects of scrambling. Sentences (3a-b) are different with respect to scope: (3b) is ambiguous with regard to the relative scope of the subject and the object, whereas (3a) is not (Hoji 1985, Kuno 1973, Kuroda 1965, 1970). The pair of Korean sentences in (4) displays the identical pattern(Sohn 1994, Ko 2018).

(4) a. Nwukwunka-ka   nwukwuna-lul   salanghanta.

someone-Nom   everyone-Acc   loves

'Someone loves everyone' (some>every, *every>some)

b. Nwukwuna-lul   nwukwunka-ka   salanghanta.

everyone-Acc   someone-Nom   loves

'Someone loves everyone' (some>every, every>some)

If scrambling is movement, the contrast in scope between the pair of sentences in (3–4) can be easily captured; movement produces two possible interpretation sites. Sentence (3b), for instance, is represented as (5) under the movement approach.

(5) [everyone–acc   someone–nom   ~~everyone acc~~   love]

If the upper copy of *nwukwuna* 'everyone' is interpreted in (3b), the 'every>some' reading is produced, and if, on the other hand, the lower copy of *nwukwuna* is interpreted, the 'some>every' reading is produced. However, this section shows that there are some empirical challenges to the movement approach to scrambling.

2.1. Multiple Scrambling and Scrambling Paradoxes

For the movement approach to be tenable, it must be complemented by the condition that scrambling across a scrambled constituent must not be permitted. Let us suppose that (3a) is generated via multiple scrambling, as illustrated in (6a–c). If so, the sentence is incorrectly predicted to be ambiguous.

(6) a. [S(ubject) O(bject) V(erb)]: Scrambling of Object

b. [O [S Θ V]]: Scrambling of Subject

c. [S [O [~~S Θ~~ V]]]

In order to prevent this unwanted result, we need to resort to a constraint like (7).[5]

  (7) No Crossing Condition (NCC): Crossing across a scrambled constituent is prohibited.[6]

Once we admit the NCC, however, we run into an immediate problem with a generation of sentences like (8b). In (8a) IO must have scope over DO. This suggests that the basic word order is 'S IO DO V'.

  (8) a. John-ga   dareka-ni   daremo-o   syookaisi-ta (Japanese)
         John-nom someone-dat everyone-Acc introduce-Past
         'John introduced everyone to someone'
         (someone>everyone; *everyone>someone)
     b. Dareka-ni   daremo-o   John-ga   syookaisi-ta
         someone-Dat everyone-Acc John-Nom introduce-Past
         'John introduced everyone to someone'
         (someone>everyone; *everyone>someone)

5　Another possibility is that string vacuous scrambling is not permitted. Scrambling of O in (6a) gives rise to word order change, and scrambling of S undoes the effect of the previous scrambling. In short, the two occurrences of scrambling is string vacuous, which may not be permitted.

6　It is not clear whether NCC applies to every type of movement. I tentatively assume that it is true of so-called optional movement.

If scrambling is subject to 'Shortest Move' and the Extension Condition, the dative phrase (i.e., IO) must move first, which is followed by the
movement of the accusative phrase (DO), as shown in (9a−b). In (9b) DO
must cross scrambled IO and in (9c) IO must cross scrambled DO: that
is, the NCC in (7) is violated twice in the derivation (9).

(9) a. S IO DO V: Scrambling of IO

b. IO S ~~IO~~ DO V: Scrambling of DO across the scrambled IO

c. DO IO S ~~IODO~~ V: Scrambling of IO across the scrambled DO

d. IO DO ~~IO~~ S ~~IODO~~ V

Even if we assume that scrambling is not subject to 'Shortest Move',
as shown in (10), there is no way to generate the string in (8b) without
violating the constraint in (7).

(10) a. S IO DO V: Scrambling of DO

b. DO S IO ~~DO~~ V: Scrambling of IO across the scrambled DO

c. IO DO S ~~IO DO~~ V

Besides the generation paradox, there is one more paradox called the
scope rigidity paradox. We have seen that movement produces an am−
biguous structure. Interestingly, however, the multiply scrambled sentence
in (8b) is not ambiguous regarding the relative scope of IO and DO, as
observed by Yatsushiro(1996). Let us say that the constraint in (7) is not

correct, and hence either the derivation in (9) or (10) is correct. Then, it is incorrectly predicted that (8b) is ambiguous. It is noteworthy that the pattern in (8a-b) is not an idiosyncratic property of Japanese. The same phenomenon is attested in Korean: IO must have scope over DO although both constituents occur in the scrambled positions.

(11) a. Tom-i   nwukwunka-eykey   nwukwuna-lul sokayha-yess-ta.
        Tom-Nom someone-Dat   everyone-Acc   introduce-Past-Dec
        'Tom introduced someone everyone' (Korean)
        (someone>everyone; *everyone>someone)

    b. Nwukwunka-eykey   nwukwuna-lul Tom-i   sokayha-yess-ta.
        someone-Dat   everyone-Acc   Tom-Nom introduce-Past-Dec
        (someone>everyone; *everyone>someone)

To sum up, the multiply scrambled sentences lead us to paradoxes if scrambling is movement.

2.2. Previous Approaches to Scrambling Paradoxes

Before investigating how the Revised Visibility Condition elucidates the scrambling paradoxes, let us first examine whether it is possible to explain them while assuming that scrambling is movement. There are two types of movement approach to scrambling: (i) scrambling is upward movement, and (ii) it is downward movement: scrambled phrases are base-generated, and undergo lowering into their thematic positions at LF. This section concludes that neither approach is a viable option.

2.2.1. Upward Movement Approaches

Let us first consider whether the tucking-in approach advocated by Richards(2001) can handle these problems while assuming that scrambling is upward movement. In the tucking-in approach it seems to be possible to generate the multiply scrambled sentence in (8b) without violating the NCC. The movement of IO in (12a-b) does not violate the NCC. Furthermore, DO does not cross the scrambled IO, but lands in a specifier to the left of the existing one that is occupied by IO.

(12) a. [S IO$_F$ DO$_F$ V]: Merger of F and Scrambling of IO (No violation of the NCC)

b. [IO$_F$ [S I̶O̶$_F$ DO$_F$ V] F]: Tucking-in of DO (No violation of the NCC)

c. [IO$_F$ [DO$_F$ [S I̶O̶$_F$ D̶O̶$_F$ V] F]]

The immediate question is how the word order 'DO IO S V' is generated in this approach. Sentences (13) and (14) are perfectly grammatical although they are in violation of the NCC.

(13) Daremo-o   dareka-ni   Tom-ga   syookaisi-ta. (Japanese)

everyone-Acc   someone-Dat   Tom-Nom   introduce-Past

(everyone>someone, someone>everyone)

(14) Nwukwuna-lul nwukwunka-eykey Tom-i   sokayha-yess-ta. (Korean)

    everyone-Acc someone-Dat   Tom-Nom introduce-Past-Dec

    (everyone>someone, someone>everyone)

With a view to generating (13-14), Richards(2001, 1997) suggests that it is generated when there are multiple attractors.

(15) a. [S IO_{F1} DO_{F2} V]: Merger of F1

    b. [[S IO_{F1} DO_{F2} V] F1]: Scrambling of IO

    c. [IO_{F1} [S ~~IO_{F1}~~ DO_{F2} V] F1]: Merger of F2 and Scrambling of DO
       (the NCC is disobeyed)

    d. [DO_{F2} [IO_{F1} [S ~~IO_{F1}~~~~DO_{F2}~~ V] F1] F2]

He proposes that the NCC is disobeyed when there are multiple attractors, and when the NCC is not obeyed, quantifier scope is affected. According to him, (13-14) are scopally ambiguous, because the NCC is violated in these sentences. The tucking-in approach appears to deal with the data in (13-14) if we make use of multiple attractors. Once we assume that there can be multiple attractors for scrambling, however, we encounter a serious problem. There is no way to block the derivation in (16): that is, 'IO DO S V' can be derived even when there are two attractors. Let us assume that DO and IO have the features F1 and F2, respectively, and that the feature F1 is attracted before F2. If this is so, the NCC is disobeyed twice.

(16) a. [S IO_{F2} DO_{F1} V]: Merger of F1

b. [[S IO_{F2} DO_{F1} V] F1]: Scrambling of DO (the NCC is disobeyed)

c. [DO_{F1} [S IO_{F2} ~~DO_{F1}~~ V] F1]: Merger of F2 and Scrambling of IO
(the NCC is disobeyed)

d. [IO $_{F2}$ [DO_{F1} [S ~~IO_{F2}~~ ~~DO_{F1}~~ V] F1] F2]

Since the NCC is violated in (16), it is predicted that DO can have scope over IO. However, this prediction is wrong; as mentioned above, the 'DO>IO' reading is not permitted when the word order is 'IO DO S V'.

Another possible solution to the scrambling paradoxes is to propose that (13–14) are instances of VP scrambling. If we make use of VP preposing, we can get the word order 'IO DO S V'(Yatsushiro 1999, Koizumi 2000, Arano 2017): it seems that (13–14) can be generated if VP can undergo scrambling and the V in the scrambled VP can be deleted.

(17) a. [[[$_{vP}$ S [$_{VP}$ IO DO V] v] T] C]: VP Scrambling

b. [$_{CP}$ [$_{TP}$ [$_{vP}$ [$_{VP}$ IO DO V] [$_{vP}$ S $_{VP}$~~IO DO V~~ v]] T] C]: V–to–v
Raising, [Vv]–to–T raising, [[V v] T]–to–C Raising

c. [$_{CP}$ [$_{TP}$ [$_{vP}$ [$_{VP}$ IO DO V] [$_{vP}$ S $_{VP}$~~IO DO V~~ V v]] [Vv T]] [V
v C]]: Deletion of V in the Scrambled VP

d. [$_{CP}$ [$_{TP}$ [$_{vP}$ [$_{VP}$ IO DO ~~V~~] [vP S $_{VP}$~~IO DO V~~ ~~V v~~]] ~~[Vv T]~~] [V
v T C]]

There are several problems with this approach, the most serious of which is that in (17d), neither IO nor DO can c-command S, and hence it is predicted that they cannot have scope over S. However, the prediction is wrong. The universal dative phrases in (18a) and (19a) and the universal accusative phrases in (18b) and (19b) can take scope over the nominative existential phrases, which would be unexpected if VP were displaced.

(18) a. Daremo-ni   Tom-o   dareka-ga   syookaisi-ta. (Japanese)
        Everyone-Dat Tom-Acc   someone-Nom   introduce-Past
        (every>some)

    b. Tom-ni   Daremo-o   dareka-ga   syookaisi-ta.
        Tom-Dat   everyone-Acc someone-Nom   introduce-Past
        (every>some)

(19) a. Nwukwuna-eykey Tom-ul   nwukwunka-ka   sokayha-yess-ta.
        everyone-Dat   Tom-Acc someone-Nom   introduce-Past-Dec
        (every>some)

    b. Tom-eykey nwukwuna-lul   nwukwunka-ka   sokayha-yess-ta.
        Tom-Dat   everyon-Acc   someone-Nom   introduce-Past-Dec
        (every>some)

To conclude, the scrambling paradoxes cannot be resolved if we assume that scrambling is upward movement.

2.2.2. Downward Movement Approach

Besides the scrambling paradoxes, there are many other problems with the upward movement approach to scrambling. Under the approach (i) it is mysterious that scrambling is optional and (ii) it is hard to find motivation for scrambling: that is, it is hard to find a feature that seems to be responsible for upward movement.[7] These considerations lead Bošković (2004) and Bošković and Takahashi(1998) to propose a downward movement approach. According to them, scrambled phrases are base-generated in the scrambled positions, and lower into their thematic positions at LF. This claim is based on the assumption that thematic roles are syntactic features and the thematic features are weak in scrambling languages.

(20) Daremo-o   dareka-ga   aisiteiru.

everyone-Acc   someone-Nom   love

(21) a. [everyone-Acc [someone-Nom [love$_{(Theme)}$]-v$_{(Experiencer)}$] Present]:

Lowering into a Thematic Position

b. [~~everyone-Acc~~ [someone-Nom [everyone-Acc love$_{(Theme)}$]-v$_{(Experiencer)}$]

Present]

Under their base-generation approach there is no problem with gener-ation of (13-14); the NCC is not violated, since both IO and DO are

---

7   Accordingly, many linguists(Kuroda 1988, Saito 1989, Fukui 1993, Saito and Fukui 1998, among others) adopt the view that scrambling is an optional movement that is not grammatically motivated. However, Miyakawa(1997, 2001, 2003, 2005) proposes that scrambling is motivated by EPP. See also Lee 1993, Grewendorf and Sabel 1999, Kitahara and Kawashima 2003, Otsuka 2005, and Sabel 2001, for a view that scram-bling requires grammatical motivation.

base-generated in the scrambled positions.[8]

Bošković and Takahashi make use of downward movement in order to ensure that the scrambled DP is assigned a thematic role. They propose that long distance scrambled DPs, that is, clause-externally scrambled DPs, must undergo LF lowering in order to be assigned a thematic role.

(22) Long Scrambling: [Scrambled DP... [CP... V$_{\text{(thematic role)}}$..]]

Lowering (Obligatory Reconstruction)

On the other hand, short-distance scrambled DPs (i.e., clause-internally scrambled DPs) sometimes undergo LF lowering but sometimes remain in their S-Structure position, for head movement obviates the need for lowering.

(23) a. Short Scrambling: [Scrambled DP... V$_{\text{(thematic role)}}$..]]

Lowering (Reconstruction)

b. Short Scrambling: [$_{\text{CP}}$Scrambled DP...V$_{\text{(thematic role)}}$..] V$_{\text{(thematic role)}}$C]

Head Movement (No Reconstruction)

---

8 However, it is unclear whether the lowering approach can deal with the scope paradox.

(i) [TP IO [TP DO [TP S [V v] T]]]

Let us suppose that IO undergoes lowering to be assigned a thematic role, whereas DO is assigned a thematic role via head movement. If so, it is incorrectly predicted that DO can have scope over IO.

They assume that V universally ends up in T by LF, and so scrambled arguments can be assigned their thematic role without lowering. This proposal appears to capture the fact that in Japanese long scrambling displays obligatory reconstruction effects, whereas short scrambling displays optional reconstruction effects; since long distance head movement is not possible, clause-externally scrambled DPs must undergo lowering, and since short distance head movement is optionally permitted, clause-internally scrambled DPs optionally undergo lowering.

There are several problems with the lowering approach. The first arises with respect to the relation between head movement and lowering. In Korean head movement is blocked by the negative morpheme an 'not' (Kang 1988, Ahn 1991, Park 1992, Hagstrom 1996). In (24a) the verb *salang* 'love' cannot move to T on account of the intervening negative morpheme *an*, as represented by (24b).

> (24) a. Nwukwunka-ka   nwukwuna-lul   salangha-ci   an-h-un-ta.
>   someone-Nom   everyone-Acc   love-CI   not-do-Pres-Dec
>   b. [[love v] not do T C]

If this is so, it is predicted that scrambled objects must undergo lowering in negative sentences.

> (25) [Object   [Subject   [love$_{(thematic\ role)}$] v] not do T C]

The prediction, however, is wrong. Let us consider (26a–b), for illustration.

(26) a. Nwukwuna–lul nwukwunka–ka salangha–ci an–h–un–ta.

everyone–Acc someone–Nom love–CI not–do–Pres–Dec

'For everyone, there is someone who does not love him'

(every>some>not)

'There is someone who everyone does not love' (some>every>not)

b. [Tom–kwa Mary]–lul [selo–uy pwumo]–to salangha–ci

[Tom–and Mary]–Acc [each other–Gen parent]–too love–CI

an–h–un–ta.

not–do–Pres–Dec

'As for Tom and Mary, even each other's parents don't love them'

There are three possible representations for (26a). If the subject occurs in the SPEC–T, the object occupies the outer SPEC of TP, and if it occurs in the SPEC–v, the object occupies either the outer SPEC of vP or the SPEC–T.

(27) a. [$_{TP}$ Object [$_{TP}$ Subject [$_{NegP}$ [$_{vP}$ [$_{v'}$ love$_{(Theme)}$ V$_{(Experiencer)}$]] not] do T]]

b. [$_{TP}$ [$_{NegP}$ [$_{vP}$ Object [$_{vP}$ Subject [$_{v'}$ love$_{(Theme)}$ V$_{(Experiencer)}$]]] not] do T]

b'. [$_{TP}$ Object [$_{NegP}$ [$_{vP}$ Subject [$_{v'}$ love$_{(Theme)}$ V$_{(Experiencer)}$]] not] do T]

Regardless of whether the object occupies the (outer) SPEC–T or the outer SPEC-v, the scrambled object cannot be associated with its thematic role without lowering, and accordingly, the lowering approach predicts that it must undergo lowering. However, this prediction is incorrect. The scrambled object can have scope over the subject in (26a), and furthermore, it can serve as a binder for *selo* 'each other' in (26b), which suggests that scrambled objects do not undergo mandatory reconstruction.

Another problem with the lowering approach is that it is not clear how lowering takes place across a phase boundary. A consensus has formed that CP is a phase, although there are various versions of phase theory(e.g. Chomsky 2000, 2001, 2008, den Dikken 2006, 2007, Bošković 2010, Takahashi 2011). If we assume that lowering is also subject to the PIC, it is not possible to lower the scrambled DP into the internal thematic role of the embedded clause; once the embedded CP is mapped into PF and LF, its internal structure is not visible. Thus, it seems that the lowering approach is not compatible with the PIC-based theory.

(28) $[_{TP}$ Scrambled DP $[_{TP}\cdots.$ $[_{CP}$ $[S$ $[S$ $[V_{(\theta\text{-role1})..}]$ $v_{(\theta\text{-role2})}$ $]$ $T]$ $C]$ V $v_{(\theta\text{-role3})}$ $T]]$

So far, we have seen that there are some empirical and conceptual problems with the downward movement approach. The downward movement approach seems to be wrong, but it is undeniable that the base-generation approach has some merits. The rest of this article shows that the Revised Visibility Condition enables us to maintain the base-generation approach while assuming that scrambling is not downward movement.

3. An Agree-Based Approach to the Scrambling Paradoxes

The order of arguments is determined by thematic roles and Case assigners. In English, for instance, thematic role assignment and Case assignment require a strict locality condition, which results in a fixed word order. This section, however, shows that neither thematic role assignment nor Case assignment requires a fixed word order if (i) the TP–adjoined position becomes a Case position via head movement of Case assigners and (ii) an argument has a specified Case value. In this approach scrambling or free word order can be produced via base–generation, because scrambled positions can be both Case positions and thematic positions.[9]

3.1. Scrambled Position as a Case Position

In any version of Case–assignment theory, Case assignment is subject to the C–command Condition: that is, a Case assigner (i) must c–command its assignee.[10] The C–command Requirement can be satisfied via head movement in Japanese and Korean. All the Case assigners can c–command all the clause–internal arguments if they undergo head movement to C(Otani and Whitman 1991, Miyagawa 1997, Koizumi 2000). Consequently, the Case assigners can c–command the TP–adjoined scrambled DPs. In (29), for

---

9   Fanslow(2001) also proposes that A–scrambling does not exist. He argues that scrambling orders are base–generated, as advocated in this paper.

10   I assume that Case is assigned via downward Agree, not via upward Agree.

instance, the verbal complex $[_C[_T[_v \, V \, v_{[+acc]}]T]C_{[+nom]}]$ c-commands all the TP-internal arguments, meeting the C-command Requirement.

(29) $[_{CP} \, [_{TP} \, DP-Acc \, [_{TP} \, DP-Nom \, \cdots] \, \cdots]] \, [_C \, [_T \, [_v \, V \, v_{[+acc]}] \, T] \, C_{[+nom]}]]$[11]

What is noteworthy is that Japanese and Korean arguments have an overt Case marker--a specified Case feature. Hence Case assigners take as their goal the closest argument with the same Case feature: i.e., Japanese and Korean do not obey the Minimality Condition. Notice that in (30) *Tom-Acc* intervenes between *Mary-Nom* and C, which is a nominative Case assigner. However, nominative Case checking can take place; Case checking takes place via the shared Case value.

(30) a. $[_{CP} \, [_{TP} \, Tom-Acc \, [_{TP} \, Mary-Nom \, [_{vP} \, [_{VP} \, love_{(theme)}] \, v_{(agent, \, acc-Case)}] \, Pres]]$

$C_{[nom]}]$: V-to-v-to-T-to-C Movement

b. $[_{CP} \, [_{TP} \, Tom-Acc \, [_{TP} \, Mary-Nom \, [_{vP} \, [_{VP} \, \overline{love}_{(theme)}][\overline{love}_{(theme)} \, \overline{v}_{(agent)}]]$

$[\overline{love}_{(theme)} \, \overline{v}_{(agent, \, acc)} \, \overline{pres}]]] \, [love_{(theme)} \, v_{(agent, \, acc)} \, Pres \, C_{[nom]}]]$

Let us recall that v-to-T head movement is blocked by the negative morpheme *an*. This phenomenon does not undermine the claim that the Case feature of the scrambled DP can be checked in the scrambled position.

11　Korean has an overt comp in the matrix clause as well as in the embedded clause. I assume that Japanese has a covert comp in the matrix clause.

(31) Mary-lul   Tom-i   salangha-ci-(lul)   an-h-un-ta

     Mary-Acc   Tom-Nom   love-CI-Acc   neg-do-Pres-Dec

If v-to-T head movement cannot take place, the verb *ha* 'do' is inserted as a last resort to avoid the Stray Affix Condition, as in English(Hagstrom 1996).

(32) a. [[salangha v] ci ani] n

     [[love v] CI Neg] T: *Ha-insertion*

   b. [[[salangha v] ci ani] ha n]

     [[love v] CI Neg HA T]: Accusative Case Assignment

   c. [[[salangha v] ci-lul ani] ha n]

     [[[love v] CI-acc Neg] ha T]

Interestingly, the inserted *ha* can check accusative Case, which is evidenced by the fact that the nominal comp *ci* can be realized with accusative Case.[12]

(33) [$_{CP}$ [$_{TP}$ Mary-lul [$_{TP}$ Tom-i [$_{NegP}$ [salangha v] ci-**lul** ani] [ha T]] [[ha-n] ta]]

[$_{CP}$ [$_{TP}$ Mary-acc [$_{TP}$ Tom-nom [$_{NegP}$ [love v] CI-**acc** Neg] [ha T]] [[ha T] C]]

---

12   *Ci* is a complementizer selected by the negative morpheme *an*.

In Korean multiple Case checking is possible: both multiple nominative constructions and multiple accusative constructions are permitted.

(34) a. Mary-Nom eye-Nom pretty $C_{[+nom]}$

  b. (Mary-nom) John-Acc   arm-Acc   hold $v_{[+acc]}$

In (33) the dummy verb *ha* can multiply check the Case feature of the nominal comp *Cl-acc* and that of *Mary-acc*.[13] Therefore, we conclude that Case assigners move to C even in negative sentences as well as in positive sentences and hence are capable of checking the Case features of TP-internal DPs.

3.2. Scrambled Position as a Thematic Position

Thus far, we have seen that the scrambled position can be a Case position. If it can be a thematic position as well, an argument can be base-generated in a scrambled position. In what follows, I explore the possibility that TP-adjoined positions can be thematic positions under the Case-as-a-probe approach. We have seen that v-to-T movement is not permitted in negative sentences, which implies that thematic role assigners

---

13 If the No Tampering Condition applies in the narrow syntax, *ha*-insertion takes place at PF, which implies that Case assignment takes place at PF, as suggested by Marantz (1991) and Harley(1995).

do not move in negative sentences. Accordingly, the TP-adjoined DPs cannot be assigned thematic roles if thematic role assignment requires a sisterhood relation.

(35) [$_{TP}$ Mary-Acc [$_{TP}$ Tom-Nom [$_{NegP}$ [love$_{(Theme)}$ v$_{(Experiencer)}$] CI Neg] do T]]

However, this section shows that they can be assigned thematic roles if Case is a probe taking a thematic role as its goal.

Let us first consider the relation between Case and a thematic role. There is no one-to-one correspondence between a Case marker and its corresponding thematic role. For instance, nominative Case can be associated with Agent or Theme, and on the other hand, Theme can be associated with nominative Case as well as accusative Case. However, it is not the case that there is no relation between a theta role and its corresponding Case at all. A Case assigner must be strictly local to its corresponding thematic role bearer. For illustration, let us consider (36). In this configuration the Case assigner v$_{(acc-Case)}$ is the closest assigner to the Theme role bearer meet$_{(Theme)}$. If so, the DP with accusative Case must be realized as the Theme of this sentence. Likewise, the argument with nominative Case must be realized as an Agent, since the nominative Case assigner is closest to the Agent role bearer.

(36) [C$_{(nom)}$ [T [v$_{([Agent, Nom], acc)}$ [meet$_{(Theme)}$]]]]

The gist of the claim is that although there is no one-to-one correspondence between Case and its corresponding thematic role, it is possible
to capture the relation between them if the syntactic configuration is
provided.

(37) a. The thematic role 1 is assigned to the DP with α Case if the Case
assigner with the feature [α] is closest to the predicate with the
thematic feature $\Theta 1$.[14]

b. The Case-assigner α is closest to the thematic role β if the former
c-commands the latter, and there is no other Case assigner or thematic
role intervening between them.

The locality relation between the Case assigner and the predicate
stipulated in (37) follows if there is a checking relation between them. Let
us recall that the Case of an argument takes a thematic role as its
sub-feature. Likewise, I propose that the thematic role of a predicate takes
Case as its sub-feature, and the value of the Case feature on the predicate

---

14 There are two types of arguments: clausal arguments and DP arguments. The clausal
arguments, unlike DP arguments, do not require Case. English Case is not selective
but distinguishes a Case-requiring thematic role from a thematic role that does not
require Case: that is, the thematic role that is assigned to a Caseless argument does
not show intervention effects. In (i), for instance, *John* takes the theme of *sick* as its
goal, although the thematic role 'proposition' is the closest thematic role; the theme
of *sick* is the closest thematic role that has a Case feature as its sub-feature.

(i) John(u-Case, u-Θ) seems(proposition) [to be sick([theme, u-Case])] is valued by the closest Case assigner.[15] In (38a) the sub-feature of the Theme role is valued as [Acc], since the closest Case assigner is the accusative Case assigner v, and the sub-feature of the Agent role is specified as [Nom] on account of the closest Case assigner C.

(38) a. $[v_{([Agent, u-Case], acc)} [meet_{([Theme, u-Case])}]]$: Valuation of [uCase] on *meet* as Acc-Case

b. $[v_{([Agent, u-Case], acc)} [meet_{([Theme, Acc])}]]$: Merger of T & C, and Valuation of [uCase] on v as Nom-Case

c. $[C_{(Nom)} [T [v_{([Agent, Nom], acc)} [meet_{([Theme, Acc])}]]]]$

Let us recall that Japanese/Korean overt Case markers have a specified Case value. If both the Case marker and the thematic role bearer have specified Case values, they can make a relation although they are not in a local relation: they are not subject to the Minimality Condition but to the Relativized Minimality Condition(Rizzi 1990, 2001, 2005).[16] In (39a), for

---

15 According to this view, the Case of a thematic role assigner makes a relation with both its corresponding Case assigner and the Case of the corresponding argument. If so, there may be no need for the Case of an argument to be checked by the Case assigner.

16 If there is an overt Case marker, it has a specified Case value. However, it is not the case that the covert marker always has an unvalued Case feature. There are two cases in which Case is not pronounced. One is a case of deletion, and the other is a case of unvalued Case. For instance, (i) is an instance of deletion.

(i) Mary, Tom-i salanghay
Mary, Tom-nom love 'As for Mary, Tom loves'

instance, $[DP_{[\alpha\text{-}Case,\ u\text{-}Theme]}]$ can take $Y_{[\Theta\ Theme,\ \alpha\text{-}Case]}]$ as its goal, although there may be an intervening DP with a different Case. The point here is that the feature complex $[\alpha\text{-}Case, u\text{-}\Theta]$ can take $Y_{[\Theta\ Theme,\ \alpha\text{-}Case]}]$ as its goal even from a long distance, since they have the identical Case feature.

(39) a. $[\underline{DP_{([\alpha\text{-}Case,\ u\text{-}\Theta])}}\ DP_{([\beta\text{-}Case,\ u\text{-}\Theta])}[\underline{Y_{([\Theta],\ \alpha\text{-}Case])}}]...]$: Thematic Role Assignment

         Probe   Goal

b. $[\underline{DP_{([\alpha\text{-}Case,\ \Theta])}}\cdots\ DP_{([\beta\text{-}Case,\ u\text{-}\Theta])}\ \cdots[\cdots\underline{Y_{([\Theta],\ \alpha\text{-}Case])}}]\cdots]$

For illustration, let us generate sentence (40). If *Tom-ga* 'Tom-nom' is merged with the string in (41a), it can be assigned the Agent role via valuation, since the sub-feature of Agent is Nominative Case.

(40) Mary-o   Tom-ga   home-ta.

     Mary-Acc   Tom-Nom   praise-Past 'Tom praised Mary'

(41) a. $[_{TP}\ [_{vP}\ [_{VP}\ praise_{([Theme,\ acc])}]\ v_{([Agent,\ Nom],\ acc)}]\ T]$: Merger of

                                           Tom-ga$_{([Nom,\ u\text{-}\Theta])}$

b. $[_{TP}\ Tom\text{-}ga_{([Nom,\ u\text{-}\Theta])}\ [_{vP}\ [_{VP}\ praise_{([Theme,\ Acc])}]\ v_{([Agent,\ Nom],\ Acc)}]\ T]$:

    Valuation of Thematic Role (Thematic Role Assignment)

c. $[_{TP}\ Tom\text{-}ga_{([Nom,\ Agent])}\ [_{vP}\ [_{VP}\ praise_{([Theme,\ Acc])}]\ v_{([Agent,\ Nom],\ Acc)}]\ T]$:

    Merger of *Mary-o*$_{([Acc,\ u\text{-}Theme])}$

In (i) *Mary* has a specified Case value, although its Case is not overtly realized.

d. [$_{TP}$ Mary-o$_{([Acc-, u-\theta])}$ [$_{TP}$ Tom-ga$_{([Nom, Agent])}$ [$_{vP}$ [$_{VP}$ praise$_{([Theme, Acc])}$]

V$_{([Agent, Nom], Acc)}$] T]]: Valuation of Thematic Role

e. [$_{TP}$ Mary-o$_{([Acc, Theme])}$ [$_{TP}$ Tom-ga$_{([Nom, Agent])}$ [$_{vP}$ [$_{VP}$ praise$_{([Theme, Acc])}$]

V$_{([Agent, Nom], Acc)}$] T]]

If, on the other hand, *Mary-o* 'Mary-Acc' is merged with the resulting structure in (41c), its feature complex [*Acc-Case, u-θ*] takes the feature complex [*Theme, Acc*] as its goal, and as a consequence, the u-θ is valued as *Theme*. According to the Relativized Minimality Condition, only the same Case can be a barrier. In (41d) the feature complex of *Mary-o* can take that of *praise* as its goal, since only the accusative Case is a barrier to the operation 'Agree'. It is also noteworthy that although vP is a phase, it is not a barrier to feature checking in (40). It is because V-to-v head movement nullifies the phasehood of vP, as den Dikken(2007) and Gallego (2010) propose. If the verb *praise*$_{([Theme, Acc])}$ moves to v, it can bear a relation with *Mary-o*$_{([Acc, Theme])}$, since the head of the vP-phase is visible from the TP-adjoined position.

(42) [$_{TP}$ Mary-o$_{([Acc, Theme])}$ ⋯ [$_{vP}$ [$_{VP}$ ~~praise~~$_{([Theme, Acc])}$] praise$_{([Theme, Acc])}$ V$_{([Agent, Nom], Acc)}$] T]

In (42) *Mary* can be assigned a thematic role from the raised copy of *praise*.

This approach does not run into the scrambling paradoxes. Let us recall that the scrambling paradoxes consist of two paradoxes: a generation paradox, and a scope rigidity paradox. If scrambling is movement, (i) it is impossible to generate the multiply scrambled sentence like (43) on account of the NCC, and (ii) there is no way to explain the fact that DO cannot have scope over IO in the sentence.

(43) Dareka-ni   daremo-o   Mary-ga   syookaisi-ta.[17]
     someone-Dat everyone-Acc Mary-nom introduce-past

The scrambling paradoxes do not arise in the approach advocated here. Since both the dative and accusative phrases are base-generated in the scrambled position, the NCC is not violated. Furthermore, it is not surprising that DO fails to have scope over IO; the scrambled positions are thematic positions and Case positions, which means that the scrambled DPs do not have to undergo raising or lowering, and consequently, the surface word order determines the scope relation.[18] [19]

Another important point is that it now becomes unsurprising that (i) scrambling is optional and (ii) it is hard to find a feature that triggers

---

[17] As suggested by an anonymous reviewer, I need to posit an applicative head for the dative case. I assume that there is an independent projection that hosts the dative phrase.

[18] The notion of 'unmarked word order' is determined on the basis of the hierarchy of the predicates: V<v<T<C.

[19] In 3.4 I argue that focalization is available in Japanese and Korean. Both focalization and scrambling produce a marked word order, but they differ with regard to reconstruction effects.

scrambling. The optionality of scrambling arises from the fact that it is possible to merge the string in (41a), repeated here as (44), either with the subject *Tom–Nom* or the object *Mary–Acc*. The string in (44) has the thematic features Theme and Agent, and there is no rule ordering that stipulates which feature must be checked first. Therefore, the scrambled word order is optionally generated.

(44) [$_{TP}$ [$_{vP}$ [$_{VP}$ praise$_{([Theme, Acc])}$] praise$_{([Theme, Acc])}$ V$_{([Agent, Nom], Acc)}$] T]

Notice that in this approach the scrambled word order is not triggered by a certain feature. Since there is no feature that triggers scrambling, it does not come as a surprise that it is hard to pin down a feature responsible for scrambling.

3.3. (Anti-)Reconstruction Effects of Short Scrambling

If short scrambling is an output of base–generation, it is not expected to permit reconstruction. Contrary to our expectation, however, the phrase in the left edge can be interpreted in a lower position than its surface position. This subsection shows that this seemingly idiosyncratic pattern arises from the fact that base–generation is not the only operation that is responsible for marked word order.

Let us first consider the straightforward case such as (45–46). In (45b) and (46b), the anaphor/pronominal contained inside the subject can be bound by the scrambled object, which suggests that scrambling displays anti-connectivity effects.

(45) a. ?*[Soitu$_i$-no hahaoya]-ga   daremo$_i$-ni   kisusi-ta. (Japanese)

      the guy-gen mother-Nom everyone-Dat kiss-Past

      'His$_i$ mother kissed everyone$_i$.'

    b. Daremo$_i$-ni   [soitu$_i$-no hahaoya]-ga   kisusi-ta.

      everyone-Dat [the guy-Gen mother]-Nom kiss-past

      'Everyone$_i$, his$_1$ mother kissed t$_i$.'

(46) a. *Caki$_i$-uy pwumo-ka   motun ai$_i$-tul-ul   honnay-ss-ta.

      self-Gen parent-Nom all   child-Pl-Acc scold-Past-Dec

      '(lit) their parent scolded all children'

    b. Motun ai$_i$-tul-ul   caki$_i$-uy pwumo-ka honnay-ss-ta.

      all   child-Pl-Acc self-Gen parent-Nom scold-Past-Dec

      'As for all children, their parents scolded them'

Anti-reconstruction effects in (45-46) are correctly predicted by the Case-as-a-probe approach, since the scrambled objects are base-generated in their surface positions, as shown in (47).

(47) a. [$_{CP}$ [$_{TP}$ everyone-Dat$_i$ [$_{TP}$ his mother$_i$-Nom [$_{vP}$ kiss$_{[Theme, Acc]}$ v$_{[Agent, Nom]}$] Past]] C]

    b. [$_{CP}$ [$_{TP}$ all children-Acc$_i$ [$_{TP}$ their$_i$ parents-Nom [$_{vP}$ scold$_{[Theme, Acc]}$ v$_{[Agent, Nom]}$] Past]] C]

The scrambled object does not have to undergo reconstruction, since it can be assigned Case and a thematic role in the scrambled position. Hence, there are no reconstruction effects in (45b) and (46b).

Surprisingly, however, the objects in (48a–b) can be interpreted in a lower position than the subjects; the anaphors inside the scrambled objects can be bound by the subjects.

(48) a. [Soitu$_i$–no hahaoya]–ni   daremo$_i$–ga   kisusi–ta.   (Japanese)

[the guy–gen mother]–Dat   everyone–Nom   kiss–Past

'his$_j$ mother$_i$, everyone$_j$ kissed t$_i$.'

b. Caki$_i$–uy   ememi–eykey   nwukwuna$_i$–ka   kisuha–yess–ta.

self–Gen   mother–Dat   everyone–Nom   kiss–Past–Dec

'his$_j$ mother$_i$, everyone$_j$ kissed t$_i$.'

The reconstruction effects in (48a–b) appear to pose a problem to the Case–as–a–probe approach; if we assume that the object is base–generated in the scrambled position, the subject fails to c–command the object.[20] This puzzling phenomenon arises from the fact that focus movement is available in Japanese and Korean as well as in English. In fact, it would be strange if scrambling languages do not permit focus movement. What is peculiar about Japanese and Korean is not that focus movement is permitted, but

---

20 Ko(2018) suggests that Korean data favors the movement approach to scrambling over the base–generation approach. This paper is eclectic in the sense that some scrambling effects arise from base–generation, where some result from movement.

that marked word order can be generated via base-generation. This article refers to the base-generation of marked word order as scrambling, and the generation of marked word order via focus movement as focalization. In short, there are two sources for marked word order in Japanese and Korean: movement and base-generation.[21] It is well-known that A'-movement like focalization shows connectivity effects. So the connectivity effects in (48a-b) can be explained if we assume that the object occupies the sentence-initial position via focalization.

> (49) a. [TP everyone-Nom [vP everyone-Nom [VP [his mother] Dat kiss] v] T]:
>   Focalization of the object
>
> b. [TP [his mother]-Dat [TP everyone-Nom [vP everyone Nom [vP [his mother] Dat kiss] v] T]]

If the lower copy is interpreted in (49b), it is not surprising that the subject can be a binder for the phrase contained in the object.[22] Therefore,

---

21 Ahn and Cho(2019) propose that there are two different types of scrambling: Adjunction and Focus Movement. Adjunction must undergo reconstruction, whereas Focus Movement does not. They assume that Focus Movement is a scope-taking movement. On the other hand, Park and Yoo(2019) claim that when scrambling takes place, there arises a labeling failure in the sense of Chomsky(2013, 2015), and there are two possible ways to fix the problem. The first strategy is to radically reconstruct the scrambled phrase, and the second is to produce a predication structure at the interface.

22 It is worthwhile to mention that we have seen that the word order 'IO DO S V' cannot be generated via upward movement if we assume that the Extension Condition is correct. That is, it is an output of base-generation. Therefore, DO fails to have scope over IO.

his can be interpreted as a bound variable.[23] To conclude, Japanese and Korean do not differ from English in that they permit focalization, but rather they are peculiar in that they permit base-generated free word order. The marked word order generated via dislocation displays reconstruction effects, although the base-generated marked word order does not.

3.4. No Crossing Condition and Merger Economy

Thus far, I have claimed that scrambling is an output of base-generation, but marked word order can be generated via base-generation or movement: that is, there are two sources for marked word order. Let us examine whether this claim runs into the problem of over-generation, by reconsidering sentences (45a) and (46a), repeated here as (50a-b).

---

23 Saito (1989, 1992) notes that the long-distance scrambled DP cannot have scope over the matrix subject in (i): the 'everyone>someone' reading is not possible in (i).

(i) Daremo-ni   dareka-ga   [Mary-ga *e* atta to]   omotte-iru. (Japanese)
   everyone-Dat   someone-Nom   [Mary-Nom met Comp] thinks
   'Everyone, someone thinks that Mary met.' (someone > everyone, *everyone > someone)
   Bošković and Takahashi (1998:354)

We can deal with (i) if we assume that long scrambling is A'-movement, as proposed by Nishigauchi(2002) and Miyagawa(1997, 2006). Admittedly, it is controversial as to whether the Korean counterpart of (i) displays the same pattern(Johnston and Park 2001:728). I leave this issue for further research.

(50) a. ?*[Soitu$_i$-no hahaoya]-ga   daremo$_i$-ni   kisusi-ta. (Japanese)

   [the guy-Gen mother]-Nom   everyone-Dat kiss-Past.

   'His$_i$ mother kissed everyone$_i$.'

b. *[Caki$_i$-uy pwumo]-ka   motun ai$_i$-tul-ul   honnay-ss-ta.

   [self-Gen parent]-Nom all   child-Pl-Acc   scold-Past-Dec

   '(lit) their$_i$ parent scolded all children$_i$' (Korean)

If both base-generation and focalization are available, it is theoretically possible that a 'SOV' word order can be generated via focalization after an 'OSV' word order is base-generated. For instance, let us say that (51) is generated along the line below:

(51) a. Daremo$_i$-ni   [soitu$_i$-no hahaoya]-ga kisusi-ta: Focalization

   [everyone-Dat [his mother]-Nom   kissed]

b. [soitu$_i$-no hahaoya]-ga daremo$_i$-ni   ~~[soitu$_i$ no hahaoya]~~-ga kisusi-ta

   [his mother]-Nom   everyone-Dat [~~his mother] Nom~~   kissed

If this derivation is permitted, it is strange that the bound variable *soitu* 'he' fails to be bound by *daremo* 'everyone'.

We need to say that once a scrambled word order is created, it must not be undone via movement: that is, we need to adopt some version of the NCC in (7), rewritten here as (52).

(52) No Crossing Condition (NCC): Crossing across a scrambled constituent is prohibited.

Let us explore the possibility of deriving the NCC from an independently motivated principle. Given the numeration in (53b), the string (54) can be merged with either $Tom\text{-}ga_{(u\text{-}Theme,\ +Focus)}$ or $Mary\text{-}o_{(u\text{-}Theme)}$.

(53) a. Tom-ga Mary-o seme-ta.

   Tom-Nom Mary-Acc blame-Past

   'Tom blamed Mary'

  b. {Tom-ga$_{([Nom,\ u\text{-}\theta],\ +Focus)}$, Mary-o$_{([Acc,\ u\text{-}\theta])}$, seme$_{([Theme,\ Acc])}$, V$_{(Agent,\ Acc)}$,

   ta, C$_{(Nom)}$}

(54) [$_{TP}$ [$_{vP}$ [$_{VP}$ blame$_{([Theme,\ Acc])}$] V$_{([Agent,\ Nom],\ acc)}$] Past]

If $Tom\text{-}ga_{([Nom,\ Agent],\ +Focus)}$ is merged with the string in (54), it must undergo further movement on account of the feature [+Focus]. On the other hand, merger with $Mary\text{-}o_{([Acc,\ u\text{-}\theta])}$ does not require further movement. I propose that merger with $Mary\text{-}o_{([Acc,\ u\text{-}\theta])}$ is more economical than merger with $Tom\text{-}ga_{(Agent,\ +Focus)}$ in that the former does not require movement whereas the latter does.

(55) Merger Economy

  All things being equal, merger with the constituent with no movement

  feature is more economical than merger with the constituent with a movement feature.

According to the Merger Economy in (55), it is more economical to merge the string in (54) with $Mary\text{-}o_{([Acc,\ u\text{-}Theme])}$ than to merge it with $Tom\text{-}ga_{([Nom,\ u\text{-}],\ +Focus)}$. Thus, merger of the string in (54) with $Tom\text{-}ga$ $_{([Nom,\ u\text{-}\Theta],\ +Focus)}$ is blocked by $Mary\text{-}o_{([Acc,\ Theme])}$. Notice that the Merger Economy prevents the derivation of the string SOSV, which is exactly what the NCC is supposed to do. It is also worthwhile to point out that the Merger Economy does not run into a look-ahead problem, because at the moment of merger the generator can decide which option would lead to a more economical derivation regardless of what operations take place later.

Let us now consider why focalization can take place in (56a).

(56) a. Mary-o   Tom-ga   seme-ta.

       Mary-Acc   Tom-Nom   blame-Past   'Tom blamed Mary'

   b. $\{Tom\text{-}ga_{([Nom,\ u\text{-}\Theta])}, Mary\text{-}o_{([Acc,\ u\text{-}\Theta],\ +Focus)}, seme_{([Theme,\ ])}, V_{(Agent,\ Acc)},$

      $ta, C_{(Nom)}\}$

If the verb $seme_{([Theme,\ Acc])}$ enters into the derivation, there are a couple of options. What is self-evident, however, is that in (57a) it cannot be merged with $Tom\text{-}ga_{([Nom,\ u\text{-}\Theta])}$ on account of the Case mismatch.

(57) a. $seme_{([Theme,\ Acc])}$: merger of $Tom\text{-}ga_{([Nom,\ u\text{-}\Theta])}$

   b. *$[_{VP}\ Tom\text{-}ga_{([Nom,\ u\text{-}\Theta])}\ seme_{([Theme,\ Acc])}]$

Accordingly, $Tom\text{-}ga_{([Nom,\ u\text{-}])}$ cannot block merger of $Mary\text{-}o_{([acc,\ u\text{-}\Theta]},$
$_{+Focus)}.$[24]

(58) a. $seme_{([Theme,\ Acc])}$: merger of $Mary\text{-}o_{([Acc,\ u\text{-}\Theta],\ +Topic)}$

b. [$_{VP}$ $Mary\text{-}o_{([Acc,\ Theme],\ +Focus)}$ $seme_{([Theme,\ Acc])}$]

To sum up, the Merger Economy prevents crossing of a thematically more prominent argument over a thematically less prominent argument.

This approach can be extended to the contrast between (59a) and (59b). Sentence (59a) is scopally ambiguous, whereas (59b) is not.

(59) a. Nwukwunka-lul nwukwuna-eykey Mary-ka   sokayha-yess-ta.

someone-Acc   everyone-Dat   Mary-Nom introduce-Past-Dec

(everyone>someone, someone>everyone)

b. Nwukwunka-eykey nwukwuna-lul Mary-ka   sokayha-yess-ta.

someone-Dat   everyone-Acc Mary-Nom introduce-Past-Dec

(someone>everyone, *everyone>someone)

This follows from the Merger Economy in (55), along with the well-

---

24 It seems that $v_{(Agent,\ Acc)}$ fails to block it either. Let us pay attention to the expression 'all things being equal'. $Mary\text{-}o_{([Acc,\ u\text{-}Theme],\ +Focus)}$ is XP, whereas $v_{(Agent,\ Acc)}$ is X. XP merger is leftward merger, whereas X merger is rightward merger. Since they are different types of merger, they are not subject to the Merger Economy: that is, it is not a violation of the Merger Economy to merge the string in (57a) with $Mary\text{-}o_{([Acc,\ u\text{-}Theme],\ +Focus)}}$, which enables topicalization to take place.

known fact that that IO is thematically more prominent than DO, as noted above. In (60a) merger of the DO *nwukwunka–lul*$_{([acc, Theme], +Focus)}$ cannot be blocked by the IO *nwukwuna–eykey*, although it has the feature [+Focus]. It is because the IO is the only argument that is compatible with *sokayha*$_{([Theme, acc])}$.

(60) a. [sokayha$_{([Theme, Acc])}$]: Merger of *nwukwunka–lul*$_{([Acc, u–\theta], +Focus)}$

b. [nwukwunka–lul$_{([Acc, Theme], +Focus)}$ sokayha$_{([Theme, Acc])}$]: A Series of Merging Operations

c. DO IO S ~~DO~~ V

The representation (60c) gives rise to scope ambiguity, depending on whether the higher copy of DO is interpreted or the lower copy is interpreted. Therefore, (59a) is ambiguous. In (61a), by contrast, merger of the IO *nwukwuna–eykey*$_{([Dat, u–\theta], +Focus)]}$ is blocked by the DO *nwukwuna–lul*$_{([acc, u–\theta])}$ in accordance with the Merger Economy.

(61) a. [[sokayha$_{([Theme, Acc])}$] V$_{Applicative([Goal, Dat])}$]: *Merger of *nwukwuna–eykey*

$_{([Dat, u–\theta], +Focus)}$

b. *[nwukwuna–eykey$_{([Dat, Goal], +Focus)}$ [[sokayha$_{([Theme, Acc])}$] V$_{Applicative ([Goal,}$

$_{Dat])}$]

Accordingly, there is no chance for the IO to be c–commanded by the DO in the course of derivation: that is, the derivation in (62) is not permitted, which means that (59b) is represented as either (63a) or (63b).

(62) *IO DO S ~~IO~~ V

(63) a. IO DO S V

b. IO DO S ~~DO~~ V

Therefore, (59b) is not ambiguous with respect to the scope interaction between IO and DO.

4. Conclusion

Arguments must bear a relation with their thematic roles. There can be two approaches to thematic role assignment if we assume that thematic roles are features. One is to assume that a thematic role requires an argument, and the other is that an argument requires a thematic role. While assuming that the second approach is the correct one, this article has proposed an AGREE-based account for thematic role assignment. There is no morphological feature for a thematic role. However, this article has proposed that Case is involved in thematic role assignment. In this account the DP with Case is a probe taking a thematic role as its goal: a Case-marked argument requires a thematic role, not the other way around. In fact, this is not a novel idea. Chomsky(1986) proposes the Visibility Condition, which stipulates that a position in a Case-marked CHAIN is visible for theta-marking. By reinterpreting the Visibility Condition under the Probe-Goal theory, I have claimed that Case is a probe and a thematic role is its goal. More precisely, the Case of an argument has an unvalued thematic role as its sub-feature, whereas the thematic role of a predicate has Case as its sub-feature, and the feature complex of the argument takes the feature complex of the predicate as its goal. This article has shown that the Case-as-a-probe approach provides a principled account of many puzzling phenomena revolving around scrambling paradoxes.

References

Ahn, H.-D. (1991), *Light Verbs, VP-Movement, Negation and Clausal Architecture in Korean and English*, Doctoral dissertation, University of Wisconsin at Madison.

Ahn, H.-D and Cho S.-E. (2019), "On Scrambling and Reconstruction," *Language and Information Society* 37, 259-286.

Arano, Akihiko. (2017), "Multiple scrambling, headless vP-movement, and Cyclic Linearization." In *NELS 47: Proceedings of the Forty-Seventh Annual Meeting of the North East Linguistic Society*: Volume 1, ed. A. Lamont and K. Tetzlof, 55-64. University of Massachusetts, Amherst: Graduate Linguistic Student Association.

Bailyn, J. F. (2001), "On scrambling: a reply to Bošković and Takahashi," *Linguistic Inquiry* 32, 635-658.

Boeckx, C., N. Hornstein, and J. Nunes. (2010), *Control as movement*. Cambridge: Cambridge University Press.

Bošković, Ž. (1994), "D-Structure, Theta Criterion, and movement into theta positions," *Linguistic Analysis* 24, 247-286.

Bošković, Ž. (2004), "Topicalization, focalization, lexical insertion, and scrambling," *Linguistic Inquiry* 35, 613-638.

Bošković, Ž. (2010), Phases beyond clauses, Ms. Univ. of Connecticut, Storrs.

Bošković, Ž. and D. Takahashi. (1998), "Scrambling and last resort," *Linguistic Inquiry* 29, 347-366.

Chomsky, N. (1981), *Lectures on Government and Binding*, Dordrecht: Foris.

Chomsky, N. (1986), *Knowledge of Language*, New York: Praeger.

Chomsky, N. (1995), *The Minimalist Program*, Cambridge, MA: MIT Press.

Chomsky, N. (2000), "Minimalist inquiry," In *Step by Step*, ed. R. Martin, D. Michaels, and J. Uriagereka, 91-155, Cambridge, MA: MIT Press.

Chomsky, N. (2001), "Derivation by phase," In *Ken Hale: A life in Linguistics*, ed. M. Kenstowicz, 1-52, Cambridge, MA: MIT Press.

Chomsky, N. (2008), On phases, In *Foundational Issues in Linguistic Theory*, ed. R. Freidin, C. Otero, and M. L. Zubizarreta, 133‒166, Cambridge, MA: MIT Press.

Chomsky, N. (2013), "Problems of projection," *Lingua* 130, 33‒49.

Chomsky, N. (2015), "Problems of projection: Extensions," In *Structures, Strategies, and Beyond: Studies in Honour of Adriana Belletti*, ed. by Di Domenico, E., C. Hamann and S. Matteini, 1‒16, Amsterdam/Philadelphia, Benjamins Publishing Company.

den Dikken, M. (2006), *Relators and linkers: the Syntax of Predication, Predicate Inversion, and Copulas*. Cambridge, MA: MIT Press.

den Dikken, M. (2007), "Phase extension: contours of a theory of the role of head movement in phrasal extraction," *Theoretical Linguistics* 33:1‒41.

Fanslow, G. (2001), "Features, theta‒roles, and free constituent order," *Linguistic Inquiry* 32, 405‒437.

Fukui, N. (1993), Parameters and optionality, *Linguistic Inquiry* 24, 399‒420.

Gallego, A. (2010), "Phase theory," Amsterdam: John Benjamins Publishing Company.

Grewendorf, G. and J. Sabel. (1999), "Scrambling in German and Japanese: Adjunction versus multiple specifiers," *Natural Language and Linguistic Theory* 17, 165.

Hagstrom, P. (1996), "Do‒support in Korean: Evidence for an interpretive morphology," In *Morphosyntax in Generative Grammar: Proceedings of the 1996 Seoul International Conference on Generative Grammar*, ed. H‒D Ahn et al, 169‒180. Seoul: Hankuk Publishing Company.

Hale, K. and S. J. Keyser. (1993), "On argument structure and the lexical expression of syntactic relations," In *The view from Building 20: Essays in Linguistics in Honor of Sylvan Bromberger*. ed. K. Hale and S. Keyser, 53‒109. Cambridge, MA: MIT Press.

Hale, K. and S. J. Keyser. (2002), *Prolegomenon to a Theory of Argument Structure*, Cambridge, MA: MIT Press.

Harley, H. (1995), *Subjects, events and licensing*, Doctoral disseration, MIT.

Hoji, H. (1985), *Logical Form Constraints and Configurational Structures in Japanese*, Doctoral Dissertation, University of Washington.

Hornstein, N. (1999), "Movement and control," *Linguistic Inquiry* 30, 69–96.

Hornstein, N. (2001), *Move! A Minimalist Theory of Construal*, Oxford: Blackwell.

Jaeggli, O. (1980), "Remarks on to-contraction," *Linguistic Inquiry* 11, 239–245.

Johnston, J. C., and I. Park. (2001), "Some problems with a lowering account of scrambling," *Linguistic Inquiry* 32, 727–732.

Kang, M.-Y. (1988), *Topics in Korean Syntax: Phrase Structure, Variable Binding, and Movement*, Doctoral dissertation, MIT.

Ko, H. (2018), Scrambling in Korean syntax, In *Oxford Research Encyclopedia of Linguistics*, ed. by M. Aronoff, New York: Oxford University Press.

Koisumi, M. (2000), "String Vacuous Overt Verb Raising," *Journal of East Asian Linguistics* 9, 227–285.

Kuno, S. (1973), *The Structure of the Japanese Language*, MIT Press: Cambridge.

Kuroda, S. Y. (1965), *Generative grammatical studies in the Japanese language*, Doctoral dissertation, MIT.

Kuroda, S. Y. (1970), "Remarks on the notion of subject with reference to words like *also*, *even*, or *only*," *Annual Bulletin of Research Institute of Logopedics and Phoniatrics* 3, 111–130.

Kuroda, S.-Y. (1988), "Whether we agree or not: A comparative syntax of English and Japanese," *Linguistic Investigations* 12, 1–47.

Lasnik, H. (1995), Last Resort and Attract F. In *Proceedings of FLSM* 6, 6281. Indiana University Linguistics Club, Bloomington.

Lee, Y-S. (1993), *Scrambling as Case driven obligatory movement*, Doctoral dissertation, Univ. of Pennsylvania.

Marantz, A. (1991), "Case and licensing," In *Proceedings of the 8th Eastern States Conference on Linguistics* (ESCOLK 8), 234–253.

Miyagawa, S. (1997), "Against optional scrambling," *Linguistic Inquiry* 28, 1–26.

Miyagawa, S. (2001), EPP, scrambling, and *wh*-in-situ, In *Ken Hale: a Life in Language*. ed. M. Kenstowicz. 293–338. Cambridge, MA: MIT Press.

Miyagawa, S. (2003), A-movement and scrambling and options without optionality, In *Word order and Scrambling*, ed. S. Karimi, 177–200. Oxford: Blackwell.

Miyagawa, S. (2005), "On the EPP," In *MIT Working Papers in Linguistics 49: Per-*

spectives on Phases. ed. M. McGinnis and N. Richards, 201–236. Cambridge, MA: MIT, Department of Linguistics and Philosophy.

Miyagawa, S. (2006), "On the undoing property of scrambling: A response to Bošković," *Linguistic Inquiry* 37, 607–624.

Nishigauchi, T. (2002), "Scrambling and reconstruction at LF," *Gengo Kenkyu* 121, 49–105.

Otani, K. and J. Whitman. (1991), "V–raising and VP–ellipsis. *Linguistic Inquiry* 22," 345–358.

Otsuka, Y. (2005), Scrambling and information focus: VSO–VOS alternation in Tongan, In *The Free Word Order Phenomenon: Its Syntactic Sources and Diversity*, ed. Joachim Sabel and Mamoru Saito, 243–280. Berlin: Mouton de Gruyter.

Park, K. (1992), *Light Verb Constructions in Korean and Japanese*, Doctoral dissertation, Univ of North Carolina at Chapel Hill.

Park, M.-K. and Yoo Y.S. (2019), "Scrambling in Korean meets the Labeling Theory," *Language and Information Society* 37, 362–391.

Richards, N. (1997), "Feature Cyclicity and (Anti–)Superiority," A Paper presented at *SCIL* 9, Eastern Michigan University.

Richards, N. (2001), *Movement in language: Interactions and Architectures*, Oxford: Oxford University Press.

Rizzi, L. (1990), *Relativized Minimality*, Cambridge, MA: MIT Press.

Rizzi, L. (2001), "Relativized Minimality effects," In *The Handbook of Contemporary Syntactic Theory*, ed. Mark Baltin and Chris Collins, 89–110. Oxford: Blackwell.

Rizzi, L. (2005), "Locality and left periphery," In *Structures and Beyond: Volume 3: The Cartography of Syntactic Structures*, ed. Adriana Belletti, 223–251. Oxford: Oxford University Press.

Sabel, J. (2001), "*Wh*–questions in Japanese: Scrambling, reconstruction, and wh–movement," *Linguistic Analysis* 31, 1–41.

Saito, M. (1989), "Scrambling as semantically vacuous A'–movement, In *Alternative conceptions of phrase structure*," ed. Mark R. Baltin and Anthony S. Kroch, 182–200. Chicago: University of Chicago Press.

Saito, M. (1992), "Long distance scrambling in Japanese," *Journal of East Asian Linguistics* 1, 69‒118.

Saito, M. (2004), "Japanese scrambling in a comparative perspective," In *Peripheries: Syntactic edges and Their effects*, ed. David Adger, Ccile de Cat, and George Tsoulas, 143‒163. Dordrecht: Kluwer.

Saito, M. and N. Fukui. (1998), "Order in phrase structure and movement," *Linguistic Inquiry* 29, 439‒474.

Sohn, K.-W. (1994), "Adjunction to Argument, Free Ride and a Minimalist Program," In *MIT Working Papers in Linguistics 24: Formal Approaches to Japanese Linguistics* I, ed. M.Koizumi and H. Ura, 315‒334. Cambridge, MA: MIT, Department of Linguistics and Philosophy.

Yatsushiro, K. (1996), "On the unaccusative construction and nominative case licensing," Generals Paper, University of Connecticut. Storrs, Connecticut.

Yatsushiro, K. (1999), Case Licensing and VP Structure, Ph. D. Thesis. University of Connecticut. Storrs, Connecticut.

Extra-linguistic knowledge and Pragmatics in the Interpretation of Korean Relative Clauses

Jaehoon Yeon

1. Introduction[1]

One of the issues in typological studies on relative clauses is the Noun Phrase Accessibility Hierarchy (NPAH). Keenan and Comrie(1977) propose the Accessibility Hierarchy (AH) as follows:

Subject (SU) > Direct Object (DO) > Indirect Object (IO) > Oblique Object (OBL) > Genitive (GEN) > Object of Comparison (OCOMP)

In Korean, relative clauses (RCs) generally follow Keenan and Comrie's

---

1   The following abbreviations are used in this paper: Abl: Ablative, Acc: Accusative particle, Dat: Dative, Dec: Declarative ending, Gen: Genitive, Imp: Imperative, Loc: Locative, Mod: Modifier, Neg: Negative, Nom: Nominative, Past: Past Tense, Pro: Reflexive Pronoun, Q: Question, Rel: Relative marker, Top: Topic.

Hierarchy, but it shows complex constraints in case of oblique objects. As in the following examples, Korean relative clauses can be formed on the first four slots in the hierarchy(Yeon 2003:38):

(1) a. Subject: [Mary-eykey   tayhak-eyse   yenge-lul   kaluchi-n] John
                    Dat   college-Loc   English-Acc   teach-Rel
                "John who taught Mary English at college"

    b. Direct Object: [John-i   Mary-eykey   tayhak-eyse   kaluchi-n]   yenge
                         Nom   Dat   college-Loc   teach-Rel   English
                    "The English which John taught Mary at college"

    c. Indirect Object: [John-i   tayhak-eyse   yenge-lul   kaluchi-n]   Mary
                           Nom   college-Loc   English-Acc   teach-Rel
                    "Mary, to whom John taught English at college"

    d. Oblique Object: [John-i   Mary-eykey   yenge-lul   kaluchi-n]   tayhak
                          Nom   Dat   English-Acc teach-Rel college
                    "The college at which John taught Mary English"

As for the fifth slot in the hierarchy, Keenan and Comrie's data show that this position can only be relativized in Korean when a pronoun is retained, as in the following example(Keenan and Comrie 1977:74):

(2) **casin-/ponin-uy**   kay-ka   chongmyenha-n ku salam
       Pro-Gen   dog-Nom   intelligent-Rel that person
    "That person whose dog is intelligent"

However, in some relative clauses, if the pronoun is retained, it becomes odd as in the following example(cf. Tagashira 1972:219, Song 1991:200).

    (3) a. [(*caki-uy) caynung-i ttwiena-n] kiho

           Self-Gen talent-Nom outstanding-Rel Keeho

           'Keeho, whose talent is outstanding'

       b. [(*caki-uy) meli-ka khu-n] Yongsu

           Self-Gen head-Nom big-Rel Yongsu

           'Yongsu, whose head is big'

In (3), if the pronoun *caki* 'self' is retained, the resulting relative clause sounds odd. Furthermore, if the context allowed appropriate interpretation, the relative clause may not contain the pronominal counterpart of the head noun as in the following example:

    (4) [(caki-uy) apeci-ka sacang-in] Yeongswu-nun ton-i manh-ta.

       self-Gen father-Nom company boss-Rel Yongsu-Top money-Nom a lot-Dec

       'Yongsu, whose father is a company boss, is rich.'

In (4), the pronominal form *caki* 'self' is optional depending on the context. If the context tells you that the fact that Yongsu's father is a company boss is well known, the relative clause does not have to retain the so-called presumptive pronoun. Here we can see first instance in which extra-linguistic knowledge and pragmatics kick in for the appropriate interpretation of Korean relative clauses.

The final slot on the hierarchy, the object of comparison, cannot be relativized in Korean(Yeon 2003:39):

(5) John-i Mary-pota khuta   →   *[John-i khu-n] Mary

      Nom   than taller   Nom taller-Rel

    "John is taller than Mary."   "*Mary who John is taller than"

Korean relative clause formation generally follows AH, but there are constraints that cannot be explicated solely based on syntactic and sematic restrictions.

2. Pragmatic constraints on the interpretation of Korean relative clauses

Although the relative clause formation in Korean generally follows Accessibility Hierarchy, it shows complex constraints in case of oblique objects. First, not all oblique NPs can be relativized. For example, the comitative NP cannot be relativized as in the following example(Lee 2017a: 82).

(6) a. *John-i   san-ey   ka-n   Mary

       Nom   mountain-to   go-Rel

"Mary, with whom John went to the mountain"

b. John-i   Mary-hago   san-ey   ka-ass-ta.

 Nom   with mountain-Loc   go-Past-Dec

"John went to the mountain with Mary."

In (6), the comitative NP Mary cannot be relativized. On the contrary, the comitative NP in (7) can be relativized(Song 1991:198).

(7) a. John-i   kyelhonha-n   Mary

 Nom   marry-Rel

 "Mary whom John married"

b. John-i   Mary-hago   kyelhonha-ess-ta.

 Nom   with   marry-Past-Dec

 "John got married with Mary."

Why is it that some comitative NP can be relativized and while some cannot? It seems that pragmatic knowledge plays an important role here. In case of (7), extra-linguistic knowledge assumes that marriage normally requires a partner, and therefore the head noun can be easily interpreted as a comitative relation of the relative clause. On the other hand, in (6) there is no such pragmatic knowledge is available(Song 1991:215).

Considering that the comitative NP in (7) is a complement, but the one in (6) is an adjunct, it could be claimed that an oblique NP can be relativized when it is a complement. However, this claim is not supported by (8) where a complement cannot be relativized(Lee 2017a:82–83).

    (8) a. *John-i Mary-lul   sam-un   myenuli[2]

           Nom   Acc   take-Rel   daughter-in-law

       "*A daughter-in-law that John took Mary as"

      b. John-i   Mary-lul   myenuli-lo   sam-ass-ta.

           Nom   Acc   daughter-in-law take-Past-Dec

       'John took Mary as a daughter-in-law.'

The oblique NP *myenuli-lo* 'as a daughter-in-law' in (8b) is a comple-ment NP that is required by the verb *sam-* 'take' in the corresponding sentence. It seems therefore not easy to specify constraints clearly when the relativization is allowed for an oblique NP.

To explain when an oblique NP can be relativized, M. Kim(2010) argues that adjunct can be relativized only when they refer to time, place, or an instrument. Consider the following examples(Kim 2010:139):

    (9) a. Mary-ka   ttena-n   kunal ohwu

          Nom leave-Rel that day afternoon

       "Afternoon on that day when May left"

---

2   An anonymous reviewer claimed that a head noun of relative clauses presupposes referentiality. (S)he claims that the reason why (8a) is ungrammatical is because the head noun *myenuli* 'daughter-in-law' is non-referential. While it is an interesting claim, I cannot wholly agree with him/her because not all the head noun of relative clauses should be referential.

    b. John-i   wuntong-ul   ha-n   wuntongcang

        Nom   exercise-Acc do-Rel playground

        "The playground in which John did exercise"

    c. apeci-ka   mwul-ul   masi-n   khep

        father-Nom water-Acc drink-Rel   cup

        "The cup with which (my) father drank water"

Kim(2010:154-155) explains that an adjunct of time, place, or instrument can be relativized because pragmatic knowledge helps to retrieve the grammatical role of the head noun. Although it is the case in most cases that locative NPs (place) can be relativized, not all place NPs can be relativized. Consider the following example, in which the place noun is marked with ablative case.

  (10) a. *[John-i o-n]   mikwuk

         Nom come-Rel   America

         'America, from which John came.'

     b. John-i   mikwuk-eyse   o-ass-ta.

         Nom   America-Abl come-Past-Dec

         'John came from America.'

It shows that not all place nouns can be relativized in Korean. As for instruments, Kim(2010) suggests that the examples in (11a) and (11b) support his argument that pragmatic knowledge helps to retrieve an instrument role of the head noun(Lee 2017a:86).

(11) a. nay-ka meystwayci-lul sanyangha-n chong

        Nom   boar-Acc   hunt-Rel   gun

       "The gun with which I hunt the boar"

b. $^?$nay-ka meystwayci-lul sanyangha-n kay

        I-Nom   boar-Acc   hunt-Rel   dog

       "The dog with which I hunt the boar"

However, the degree of acceptability differs depending on the head noun in (11).

Why is it the case that some oblique NPs can be relativized while other oblique NPs cannot? The postposition deleted along with the relativized NP in the relative clause in (11) is the instrumental marker, *-(u)lo* 'with, by means of'. What is it that helps retrieve the instrument relation in the construal of (11)? It is pragmatics (or extra-linguistic knowledge) against which the 'missing' relation between the actor's action and the NP in question is construed(Song 1991:213). Based on extra-linguistic knowledge, the most likely relation between the act of someone's hunting a boar and a gun is that of instrument. This is indeed the way how extra-linguistic knowledge and pragmatics play such an important role in the recovery of the missing relation for the appropriate construal of relative clauses. Kim (2010:155) also argues that it is pragmatic knowledge that makes (11a) acceptable but (11b) questionable. Pragmatic knowledge ensures that a gun is an instrument of hunting. The head noun in (11b), however, can be interpreted as an agent, which makes it difficult to retrieve the grammatical role of the head noun as an instrument.

In Korean, pragmatics and extra-linguistic knowledge thus play an important role in RC formation and the way in which a relative clause is interpreted. Korean relative clauses can be formed even when the head noun plays no grammatical role in the relative clause if pragmatic knowledge helps to interpret the relative clause(Song 2001:231-232, Yeon 2012).

> (12) kwika-ka   nuceci-nun   kyooysaynghwal
>
>   going home-Nom   be late-Rel   surburban life
>
>   "Suburban life such that (people) go home late"

An understanding of suburban life, where people might take more time to get home from a downtown workplace, makes the construal of the relative clause in (12) possible.

We can also provide examples below to show how pragmatic knowledge affects the acceptability of relative clauses; (13a) is acceptable while (13b) is not (Yeon 2012:443-445).

> (13) a. hwacangsil-ey   ka-l swu eps-nun   yensokkuk
>
>   toilet-Loc   go-cannot-Rel   soap drama
>
>   "A soap drama such that (people) cannot go to a toilet (while they are watching it)"

b. $^{??}$hwacangsil-ey   ka-l swu eps-nun   yenphil

    toilet-Loc   go-cannot-Rel   pencil

"$^{??}$A pencil such that (people) cannot go to a toilet"

When a soap drama is very interesting people keep watching it even when they want to go to a toilet so as not to miss a scene. Therefore (13a) can be appropriately interpreted as a legitimate noun-modifying clause. On the contrary, (13b) is not interpretable unless a very special situation is set for it, since it is generally difficult to think of a situation where people cannot go to a toilet because of a pencil. Korean relative clauses have been regarded as something special because extra-linguistic knowledge and pragmatics are critical to form and interpret relative clauses(Song 1991, 2001, Mun 2012, Yeon 2012). The peculiarities of Korean relative clauses can only be explained based on extra-linguistic knowledge and pragmatic factors. These peculiar Korean relative clauses have been studied as gapless relative clauses by some scholars(Cha 2005, Lee and Lee 2012, and Yeom (2015, 2017) among others). There have been attempts to explicate peculiarities of Korean gapless relative clauses in formal terms, but they have not been successful, which we will briefly review in the following section.

3. Attempts for a Formal Interpretation of Gapless Relative Clauses in Korean

Korean has the so-called gapless relative clauses (GRCs), which have been focus of attention recently(Cha 2005, Lee & Lee (2012), Yeom (2015, 2017)). GRCs do not have a syntactic gap in the relative clause, and therefore it is hard to explain the syntactic and semantic relation between the head noun and the adnominal clause. Consider the following examples.

(14) [sayngsen -i   tha-nun] naymsay

      fish-Nom burn-Rel   smell

      "the smell of fish-burning'   (Cha 2005:15)

(15) [thayphwung-i cinaka-n] huncek

      typhoon-Nom pass-Rel   trace

      "the trace left after a typhoon hit'   (Cha 2005:15)

(16) [apeci-ka   so-lul   phal-n] ton

      father-Nom ox-Acc sell-Rel money

      'the money obtained by father's selling an ox'

                                        (Lee and Lee 2012:204)

Cha(2015) claims that the GRC has a unique semantic property that a cause and effect relation holds between the adnominal clause and the head noun. In similar vein, Lee and Lee(2012:204) agreed that "there exists a semantic cause-effect relation holding between the GRC and its modifying head noun: the content of the adnominal GRC constitutes cause and the denotation of its head noun effect." They claim that for the coherent interpretation in GRCs like (16), the required cause-effect relation should be fully realized by the addition or coercion of a verb like *pel*-'earn' as in (16').

(16') [apeci-ka   [[so-lul   phal-a]   [pel-n]]   ton

father-Nom   ox-Acc   sell   earn-Rel   money

'the money that father earned by selling an ox'

(Lee and Lee 2012:205)

They then claim that in (16) a limited set of verbs can appear in place of *pel*- 'earn' including verbs like *malyenha*- 'prepare', *mantul*- 'make', *pat*- 'receive; all these verbs share the basic meaning of 'obtaining (money as a result of selling an ox in a given context)'. They further extend their analysis to the following seemingly controversial contrast. (Lee and Lee 2012:209)

(17) a. [apeci-ka   so-lul   pal-a   kaph-un]   ton

father-Nom ox-Acc sell   pay.back-Rel money

'the money that father paid back by selling an ox.'

b. *[apeci-ka   so-lul phal-a   kkwu-/ilh-un]   ton

father-Nom ox-Acc sell   borrow-/lose-Rel   money

'the money that father borrowed/lost by selling an ox'

Their argument is that in (17a) the cause-effect relation indirectly holds between the causing event *so-lul phala* 'selling an ox' and the following additional verb *kaph-* 'pay back' by the mediation of the verb *pel-* 'earn' as in (17') (Lee and Lee 2012:209).

(17') [apeci-ka   [[so-lul   phal-a]   [pel-e]   [kaph-]]-un]   ton

        father-Nom ox-Acc   sell   earn   pay.back-Rel money

        'The money that father paid back by selling an ox and thereby earned'

According to Lee and Lee(2012:206), in (17b), however, "the verbs *kkwu-* 'borrow', *ilh-* 'lose' do not constitute a natural effect of the causing event, *so-lul phala* 'selling an ox' so there arises a conflict in the information structure". Therefore, they claim that these verbs cannot be licensed here. However, this is not true, and these verbs can be interpreted well if appropriate contexts are given. For example, in case of *kkwu-* 'borrow' in (17b), suppose that the money father wanted to borrow was too much, and the lender wanted some kind of deposit or warranty goods. Therefore, father sold his ox to the lender for warranty or to make up for the shortfall, then (17b) can be appropriately interpreted as a gapless relative clause. In case of *ilh-* 'lose' in (17b), we can suppose the following situation. Father sold the ox very cheaply compared to normal market prices, and consequently he lost money in real terms. In that case, the sentence can be interpreted properly as for intended meaning. We can see therefore Korean GRCs cannot be interpreted solely based on cause-effect relations or any well-defined semantic terms. Rather pragmatics and context play crucial roles in the interpretation of GRCs.

Another problem is that as Yeom(2017) pointed out, neither Cha(2005) nor Lee and Lee(2012) deals with more tricky cases of GRCs such as (18) below:

(18) meli-ka   cohaci-nun   chayk
     brain-Nom get.better-Rel book
     'a book such that a person who reads it gets smarter'

(Yeom 2017:297)

To interpret this GRC, we need to rely on pragmatic and extra-linguistic knowledge which cannot be easily formalized in syntactico-semantic terms. In an effort to formalize the meaning of GRCs, Yeom(2017) adopts Generative Lexicon Theory proposed by Pustejovsky (1995, 2005) and tries to formalize what mechanisms can distinguish acceptable GRCs from un-acceptable ones. Yeom(2017:313) argued that "to get smarter, the possessor needs to read the book and the event of reading is involved in the Telic qualia in the meaning specification of *chayk* 'book'". He then claims that reading a book can be related to a situation that the reader gets smarter. The following is his formal representation:

(19) (Yeom 2017:313)

$\llbracket$ meli-ka   cohaci-nun $\rrbracket$ = $\lambda w \lambda s \exists x \exists y [s \sqsubseteq w$ & $brain_w(y,x)$ & become.

smart$_w$(s,x)]

$\llbracket$ chayk $\rrbracket$ = $\lambda w\lambda x[book_w(x)]$

$\llbracket$ meli-ka cohaci-nun   chayk $\rrbracket$ = $\lambda w\lambda z \exists s \exists e \exists e' \exists x \exists y[s \sqsubseteq w$ &

brainw (y,x) & become.smart$_w$(s,x) & book$_w$(z) & READw(e,x,z)]

Apart from the technicality of formalization, establishing cause and effect relations and formalization of the interpretation are already quite complex and tricky. The further problems are that there are many more complicated examples that involve more complex processes of interpretation. Consider the following example(Yeom 2017:314).

(20) son-ul   an   ssis-eto-toy-nun   kansik

hand-Acc   not   wash-may-Rel   snack

'snakcs such that a person who eats them with a hand does not have to wash the hand' (sic) (intended meaning: Here is a snack that you don't have to wash your hands in order to eat.)

In this case, we need to connect snacks and situations in which we do not need to wash our hands. To deal with such cases in Generative Lexicon Theory, they need to consider more meaning components in the meaning specifications of the head noun. This would be very complicated, and we don't know how to formulate this interpretation in formal semantic terms. As Yeom(2017:315) admits, it cannot be dealt with the secondary quale formally. Yeom(2017:315) failed to give the general interpretation pattern for this case, and conceded that this issue is "beyond the scope" of his paper. In order to properly interpret GRCs, we need to fill up some missing links between the situation described by the adnominal clause and the head noun. Although some missing links can be explained by the mechanisms provided by formal semantic devices, it is not possible to provide a coherent and successful interpretation for all the GRCs. As can be seen, Korean relative clauses including GRCs cannot successfully be interpreted, let alone formalized in semantic mechanisms, without considering pragmatic factors and extra-linguistic knowledge.

4. Peculiarities of Korean relative clauses

What should be particularly noted in understanding Korean relative clauses is that the relative clauses in Korean is significantly affected by not only syntactico-semantic information but also pragmatic and contextual information. In Korean, even if they are well-formed morpho-syntactically, they may not be properly interpreted if the pragmatic situations are not fully framed. Furthermore even if they have the same structure, they can be interpreted differently depending on the head noun (see section 5). In this respect, the typology of relative clauses can be categorized as a language in which syntactic hierarchy plays an important role and a language in which pragmatics plays a crucial role in formation of relative clauses.[3] The following sentence, for example, shows the characteristics of the Korean relative clauses that are different from those of the European languages.

(21) pismul-i changmun-ul   twutuli-nun   soli

rain-Nom window-Acc   hit-Rel   sound

'The sound of rain tapping the window'

Here, the head noun *soli* 'sound' shows the characteristics of Korean head nouns that do not have a coreferential NP in their relative clauses, like the gapless relative clauses of European languages. There are many gapless relative clauses in Korean, which should be interpreted as attributive clauses as follows:

(22) a. kwika-ka   nuceci-nun   kyooysaynghwal

going home-Nom be late-Rel   surburban life

"Suburban life such that (people) go home late"

b. son ssis-ul   philyo-ka eps-nun umsik-ulo   mek-upsita.

hand wash-Rel need-Nom not-Rel food-Inst   eat-let's

'Let's eat food that we don't have to wash our hands in order to eat.'

c. opaithuhaci   anh-nun   swul-lo   ha-psita.

vomit   Neg-Rel   alcohol-Inst do-let's

'Let's drink alcohol that does not make us vomit.'

---

3   It may be pointed out that distinguishing relative clauses from attributive clauses separately in a language such as Korean is a biased viewpoint influenced by European languages.

(22b) and (22c) can be treated as constituent omissions as follows:[4]

(23) b. [(mek-ki cen-ey/mek-ki wuyhayse) son ssis-ul

eat-Noml prior-Loc/eat-Noml for hand wash-Rel

philyo-ka eps-nun] umsik

need-Nom not-Rel food

'food that you don't have to wash your hands (before you eat/in order

to eat)'

c. [(masi-ko nase) opaithuha-ci anhnun] swul

drink-after vomit-Neg-Rel alcohol

'alcohol that does not make you vomit after (you) drink'

However, not all GRCs can be treated as omissions. Furthermore, Korean relative clauses are not always derived from free-standing sentences. Consider the relative clause in (22c) again.

(22c') obaithuhaci anh-nun swul

vomit Neg-Rel alcohol

(a) Alcohol that doesn't vomit.

(b) Alcohol that does not make you vomit.

---

4 A similar example can be found in English ((Matsumoto (1989:233), Song (1991:213)): e.g. Here is a snack that you don't have to wash your hands (cf. Here is a snack that you don't have to wash your hands in order to eat.)

Although the clause seems to literally mean (a), our knowledge of the world tells us that, as alcohol cannot vomit itself but can certainly make you vomit, the correct interpretation of the sentence is (b). The clause contains no causative element akin to the "make" in the English translation. As Korean has a productive system of analytical causation, this clearly shows that the relative clause is not derived directly from the corresponding free-standing sentence (24a), which is nonsensical. To express the idea of alcohol not making you vomit in a simple sentence, the causative auxiliary verb *-key ha-* is required as in (24b):

(24) a. $^?$i   swul-un   opaithuhaci   anh-nun-ta..

　　　this alcohol-Top   vomit   　Neg-Pres-Dec

　　　"$^?$This alcohol doesn't vomit."

　　b. i   swul-un   　opaithuha-key ha-ci anh-nun-ta,

　　　this alcohol-Top   vomit-Caus   　　Neg-Pres-Dec

　　　"This alcohol does not make (you) vomit."

Although the two-sentence combination may go some way to explaining relativization in English transformational grammar, it is clearly insufficient in describing Korean relative clauses.

In addition, there are a lot of relative clauses in Korean, in which a pragmatically appropriate element is chosen as a head noun while an obligatory argument in the sub-categorized structure of the verb is not selected as a head noun, as in the following example. These sentences cannot be explained by the definition of relative clauses as in European languages. In other words, the pragmatic factor is more important than the argument structure.[5] For example, suppose that you utter a sentence (25) to a friend who is wanting to buy an expensive smart phone(cf. Matsumoto 1990:121).

(25) sa-l   ton-i   iss-eyo?

buy-Rel money-Nom have-Q

"Do you have money to buy (it/one)?

(Lit: Do you have money (with which) (you can) buy (it/one)?"

In (25), the obligatory argument of the verb *sa-* 'buy' is absent, but the intended meaning is easily achieved in the given context. This can be contrasted with (25') in which the subcategorized argument *mulken* 'things' is present:

(25') sa-l   mulken-i   iss-ni?

buy-Rel thing-Nom   have-Q

'Do you have things to buy?'

---

5   In Korean, relative clauses that violates the so-called "Island Constraint" are also possible (H. Shin 1994).

(e.g.) [[e   e pintayttek-ul mek-un] sinsa-ka   may-lul mac-un] yolicip
            pancake-Acc eat-Rel gentleman-Nom stick-Acc hit-Rel restaurant
     'The restaurant in which the gentleman was hit who ate pancake (there)'

There are many constructions in Korean that cannot be explained solely on the subcategorization of the predicate. Consider the following examples (cf. Matsumoto 1990):

(26) a. Mek-un   kulus-un   kkaykkusi   ssis-ela

eat-Rel   bowl-Top   neatly   wash-Imp

"Please wash the bowls (with which) you have eaten."

b. ecey   mek-un   siktang-un   acwu   pissa-ta

yesterday eat-Rel restaurant-Top very expensive-Dec

'The restaurant where we ate yesterday is very expensive.'

In both (26a) and (26b), the object arguments of the verb *mek-* 'eat' are absent, but the intended meaning is easily achieved in the given context. Since Korean does not require all subcategorized arguments to be present in a sentence, the head-noun in the relative clause can be interpreted based on interlocutor's pragmatic knowledge. The acceptability of relative clauses under a certain interpretation depends not only on consideration of the syntactic structures but also on various pragmatic factors such as the context, background knowledge and conversational principles.

As shown in the examples above, we can see that there are special pragmatic and extra-linguistic constraints involved in the interpretation of the relative clauses with the non-argument head nouns. This also applies to the interpretation of the gapless relative clauses. Considering the characteristics of Korean relative clauses, we will look more closely at how the pragmatic and contextual factors interact to play essential roles in interpreting Korean relative clauses.

5. Importance of Context and Pragmatic Knowledge in the Interpretation of Korean Relative Clauses

The acceptability and interpretation of Korean relative clauses heavily rely on semantic, pragmatic, and extra-linguistic factors. Establishing appropriate context is especially vital in Korean. Korean does not require all complements of a predicate to be realized in a sentence and therefore allows relative clauses with multiple possible meanings. The following is an example of some possible interpretations between the head noun and relative clauses. (Matsumoto 1990:115, 1996, Yeon 2012):

(27) [[chayk-ul sa-n] haksayng]

book-Acc bought-Rel student

(a) the student (who) bought a book

(b) the student (from whom) (someone) bought a book

(c) the student (for whom) (someone) bought a book

The translation in (27a), in which the subject of the predicate is the target of relativization, may seem the most likely interpretation. However, when the relative clause is embedded in a sentence such as (28), the interpretation would almost certainly be as in (b):

(28) Chayk-ul   sa-n   haksayng-hantheyse   sacen-to   sa-ss-ta.

book-Acc buy-Rel student-from   dictionary-too buy-Past-Dec.

(a) $^?$(I) also bought a dictionary from the student who bought the book.

(b) (I) also bought a dictionary from the student from whom (I) bought
    a book.

Similarly, in a context in which someone has been buying various gifts
for students, (27) could also be used to convey the interpretation given in
(27c). Given the right context, the so-called ungrammatical Korean relative
clauses that have been rejected by some scholars can be fully acceptable.
Na(1986:139) argued that the following sentence was ungrammatical because
the direct object position in the relative clause is not filled.

(29) *[Ann-i   kkakka   cwu-n]   salam

        Nom   peel   give-Rel person

    'the person (for whom) Ann peeled (something)'

However, it can be fully acceptable given the right context. For example,
as Song(1991:217) rightly pointed out, if we suppose that people are
engaged in "a game of peeling for their friends as many apples as possible
in a given time", we can share extra-linguistic knowledge that apples are
being peeled in the game. Given the circumstances, the sentence (29) can

be interpreted appropriately. Na(1986:140) further takes the following sentence as almost unacceptable because semantically entailed position, which is beneficiary(i.e. for X), is unfilled.

(30) [??][Mary-ka　sakwa-lul　kkakka　cwu-n]　khal

　　　　Nom　　apple-Acc　peel　　give-Rel　knife

　　　'the knife (with) which Mary peeled an apple (for X)'

Again, it can be fully acceptable given the right context. Consider the following sentence(Song 1991:217).

(31) [cinanpen　Mary-ka　　sakwa-lul　　kkakka　cwu-n]　khal-ul

　　　last time　　　Nom　apple-Acc　peel　　give-Rel knife-Acc

　　　etita　　twu-ess-ni?

　　　where　place-Past-Q

　　　'Where did you put the knife with which Mary peeled apples (for you) last time?'

In (31), the context tells you that the beneficiary is the hearer and that Mary peeled apples for the hearer last time. Here again, given the right context, grammatically marginal relative clauses can be fully interpreted based on pragmatic knowledge.

The following example shows a case in which the grammatical role of the head noun is not determined by the obligatory argument of the verb.

Suppose you ask the following question to a friend who wants to buy expensive jewelry, which is repeated from above with a slight modification.

> (32) sa-l   ton-to   eps-umyense   mwel   kulehkhe po-ni?
>
> buy-Rel money-even have.not-while what like.that   see-Q
>
> 'What are you looking at like that while you have no money to buy (it) (with)?'

In the example, the verb *sa-* 'buy' as a transitive verb requires a direct object as a core argument, but in this case, *ton* 'money' is not an object but an adjunct with an instrumental role. Thus, it is important to consider the context and pragmatic information when interpreting the Korean relative clauses, since the grammatical role of the head noun cannot be determined by only the subcategorization information of the verb. In other words, the determination of the grammatical role on the target of the relativization does not crucially depend on the subcategorization of the predicate in the relative clause. The following example shows that these pragmatic information sometimes extend to extra-linguistic knowledge as follows:

> (33) Kim sensayng-i   sa-n   paykhwacem-i   eti-eyo?
>
> Kim-teacher-Nom buy-Rel   dept.store-Nom where-is
>
> (a) Where is the department store (which) Mr Kim bought?
>
> (b) Where is the department store (in which) Mr Kim bought (it)?

There are two interpretations of this sentence. The choice between (33a) and (33b) largely depends on the interlocutors' knowledge about Mr. Kim and about the place. If the interlocutors assume that Mr. Kim cannot afford to buy the department store, the preferred interpretation would be (33b), whereas if he was a millionaire or a property developer, (33a) can be a possible interpretation. A comparison of the following examples makes it clearer to understand these characteristics.

(33') Samseng-i   sa-n   paykhwacem-i eti-eyo?

Samsung-Nom buy-Rel   dept.store-Nom where-is

'Where is the department store (which) Samsung bought?'

(33'') ku pokpwuin-i   sa-n   ttang-i   eti-eyo?

the property developer buy-Rel real estate-Nom where-Dec

'Where is the real estate (which) the property developer bought?'

Since both *samseng* 'Samsung' and *pokpwuin* 'property developer' in the above two examples have an ability to purchase department stores or the real estate, the interpretation as in (33a)-type is more natural than (33b)-type. This shows that different interpretations are potentially available in Korean depending on the possible pragmatic relationship between the head noun and the relative clause.

The pragmatic relationship between the head noun and the relative clause must be plausibly related. This 'plausibility' can be loosely defined as the condition[6] that the participants of the dialogue can establish through the knowledge of the world and background information. For example, (34a) is a plausible scenario and can thus be interpreted properly, but (34b) is not plausible and cannot be interpreted unless a very special scenario is set up.

(34) a. hwacangsil-ey   ka-l swu eps-nun   yensokkuk

         toilet-to   go-cannot-Rel   soap drama

   "A soap drama such that (people) cannot go to a toilet (while they are watching it)"

   b. ^{??}hwacangsil-ey   ka-l swu eps-nun   yenphil

         toilet-to   go-cannot-Rel   pencil

   "^{??}A pencil such that (people) cannot go to a toilet"

It is important to note that in order to successfully interpret relative clauses, extra-linguistic knowledge plays an important role, i.e. information given in the context or information about the participants in the sentence shared among the participants.

Relative clauses are closely related to topic constructions(Kuno 1973, Yang 1975, Lee 1975, M. Kim 2010, J. Lee 2017a, b). In addition to formal features that are common in between relative clauses and topic constructions, they share a functional/pragmatic feature as well. Consider the following example:

---

6   The 'plausibility' condition can be comparable to 'aboutness' condition in topic con-
    structions (Kuno 1973). Korean relative constructions exhibit parallelism with topic
    constructions as discussed below.

(35) a. enehak-un   chwicik-i   elyep-ta

linguistics-Top finding a job-Nom   difficult-Dec

'As for linguistics, finding a job is difficult.'

b. chwicik-i   elyep-un   enehak

finding a job-Nom difficult-Rel linguistics

'Linguistics that is hard to find a job'

In (35a) *enehak* 'linguistics' is the topic, and it is followed by the comment that is an observation/description about the topic. The 'aboutness' is the requirement that allows topic constructions. This aboutness condition can be comparable to 'plausibility' condition in relative clauses, which is a requirement that allows an appropriate interpretation of Korean relative clauses, especially the so-called 'gapless' relative clauses. Relative clauses can be compared to a comment, and the head-noun can be compared to the topic.

Kim(2010) and Lee(2017a) also argue that there are similarities between relativization and topicalization. In Korean, what can be topicalized can be relativized as well. Consider the following examples:

(36) (cf. 6)

a. John-i   Mary-hago san-ey   ka-ass-ta.

Nom   with   mountain-Loc go-Past-Dec

'John went to the mountain with Mary.'

b. Topicalization: *Mary-nun   John-i   san-ey

Top   Nom   moumtain-Loc

ka-ass-ta.

go-Past-Dec

c. Relativization: *John-i   san-ey   ka-n   Mary

Nom mountain-Loc go-Rel

(37) (cf. 7)

a. John-i   Mary-hago   kyelhonha-ess-ta.

Nom   with   marry-Past-Dec

'John got married with Mary."

b. Topicalization: Mary-nun John-i kyelhonha-ess-ta.

Top   Nom marry-Past-Dec

"As for Mary, John got married

(with her)."

c. Relativization: John-i   kyelhonha-n   Mary

Nom   marry-Rel

"Mary who John got married"

(36-37) show that if Mary can be topicalized, it can become a head-noun of the relative clause. This parallelism can be applied to all the relative clauses discussed so far as well as examples below. The following examples are Korean gapless relative clauses that cannot be interpreted solely based on syntactic information but can be interpreted with extra-linguistic information. As seen below, they all can be topicalized as well.

(38) a. khi-ka khu-nun wuyu

   height-Nom grow-Rel milk

   "Milk that makes you grow fast"

  b. i wuyu-nun khi-ka   khu-n-ta.

   this milk-Top height-Nom grow-Pres-Dec

   "As for this milk, it makes you grow fast (if you drink it)."

(39) a. tali-ka kile poi-nun paci

   leg-Nom long look-Rel trousers

   'Trousers that make your leg look longer'

  b. i paci-nun   tali-ka kile poi-n-ta.

   this trousers-Top leg-Nom look long-Pres-Dec

   "As for this trousers, they make your legs look longer (if you wear it)."

(40) a. meli-ka cohaci-nun umsik

   brain-Nom get.better-Rel food

   'Food that make you clever'

  b. i umsik-un meli-ka cohaci-n-ta.

   this food-Top brain-Nom get.better-Pres-Dec

   "As for this food, it makes you clever (if you eat them)."

(41) a. elkwul-i yeppeci-nun seymyenpep

   face-Nom get-pretty-Rel face-washing methods

   'Face-cleansing methods that make you look prettier'

  b. i seymyenpep-un elkwul-i yeppeci-n-ta.

   this face-cleansing methods face-Nom get.pretty-Pres-Dec

   "As for this face-cleansing method, it makes you look prettier (if you use it)."

These examples are difficult to be translated into English because the head noun is not an argument of the preceding adnominal clause. The correlation shows that relative clauses are closely related to topic construc- tions in Korean. Consider some more examples, which exhibit correlations between gapless relative clauses and topic constructions.

(42) a. sopangswu-ka   chwultonghay-ya ha-l   pwul
        firefighters-Nom   dispatch-must-Rel   fire
        'Fire that firefighters needed to be dispatched (to extinguish it)'

    b. i   pwul-un   sopangswu-ka   chwultonghay-ya ha-nta.
        this fire-Top firefighters-Nom dispatch-must-Dec
        'As for this fire, firefighters need to be dispatched (to extinguish it).'

(43) a. swulikong-ul   pwulu-eya ha-l   kocang
        repairman-Acc   call-must-Rel   fault
        "Fault that a repairman needs to be called (to fix it)'

    b. i   kocang-un   swulikong-ul   pwulu-eya ha-nta.
        this fault-Top repairman-Acc   call-must-Dec
        'As for this fault, repairman needs to be called (to fix it).'

Having considered a large number of Korean relative clauses that can be topicalized, we tentatively assume that there is a close relationship between 'aboutness' condition in topic construction and 'plausibility' condition in relative clauses. It should be noted, however, that there are some topic constructions that cannot be relativized. Consider the following examples:

(44) a. sayngsen−un   mineylal−i   phwungpwuha−ta.

   fish−Top   mineral−Nom   rich−Dec

   'As for fish, there are various minerals in them.'

   b. mineylal−i   pwungpwuha−n   sayngsen

   mineral−Nom   rich−Rel   fish

   'Fish that contains various minerals'

(45) a. sayngsen−un   taykwu−ka   masiss−ta.

   fish−Top   cod−Nom   delicious−Dec

   'As for fish, cod is delicious.'

   b. *taykwu−ka   masiss−nun   sayngsen

   cod−Nom   delicious−Rel   fish

   '*Fish that cod is delicious'

In (44), what is given in the comment phrase applies to the whole denotation of the topic NP. The topic NP in (45), however, exhibits a different characteristic from one in (44). The fact that cod is delicious is not a characteristic that can be shared among all the entities under the domain of fish. In this case, the topic cannot become a head noun of relative clauses. When the information described in the comment cannot be applied to the whole entity of the topic, the topic NP cannot be relativized into a relative clause(Lee 2017b:209).[7]

6. Pragmatic factors working in the interpretation of Korean relative clauses

In this section, we will examine what kind of pragmatic information interact for appropriate interpretations of Korean relative clauses.

6.1. Correlations between head-nouns and verbs

Firstly, we can consider the correlations between the head-nouns and the verbs in relative clauses.

(46) a. [[X-ka   mek-un]   Y]

        Nom   eat-Rel

    'Y (which) X ate' (Y: food or something edible)

  b. [[X-lul   sa-n]   Y]

        Acc buy-Rel

    'Y (who) bought X' (Y: purchaser)

  c. [[X-ka   Y-lul   manna-n]   Z]

        Nom   Acc   meet-Rel

---

7   See Lee (2017b) for further discussion on (in)compatibility between relative clauses and topic constructions.

'Z (at/in which) X met Y' (Z: place or time)

In the case of normal circumstances in which special pragmatic factors do not intervene, the head-nouns are mostly likely to be obligatory arguments of the verbs in the relative clauses. In general, 'eat' requires a food, and 'buy' requires a buyer or a list of articles as a head-noun as in (47).

(47) a. Yongsu-ka   mek-un   umsik

        Nom   eat-Rel   food

   'Food that Youngsu ate'

b. chayk-ul   sa-n   salam

   book-Acc buy-Rel person

   'the person who bought the book'

However, if a special noun is used as a head-noun, it may affect the interpretation of relative clauses. For example, if a semantically awkward noun is used as a head-noun as in (48), it may be required to assign a special interpretation to match it.

(48) a. Yongsu-ka   mek-un   kulus-ul   ssis-ess-ta.

        Nom   eat-Rel   bowl-Acc   wash-Past-Dec

     'Youngsu washed the bowl in/with which he ate (food).'

b. nay-ka chayk-ul sa-n   cakka-ka   sang-ul

   I-Nom book-Acc buy-Rel author-Nom award-Acc

pat−ass−ta.

receive−Past−Dec

'The author whose book I bought received an award.'

The above sentences are cases in which the head−noun requires a special semantic and pragmatic relationship with the verb in relative clauses, and therefore it affects the interpretation of the relative clause. Under the circumstances, the head−noun is not interpreted as an obligatory argument of the verb but tends to be interpreted as a non−argument that receives an appropriate pragmatic interpretation. In the case of (48a), the inter− pretation of 'to eat (food) in/with a bowl' is much more natural pragmati− cally than an interpretation, 'to eat a bowl'. (48b) is also a grammatically awkward sentence, but it can be interpreted nicely as shown in the example given a pragmatic context.

In prior research, particularly in formal syntax, the pragmatic factors have been neglected in the research on relative clauses. Considering that the pragmatic factors play important roles in the interpretation of Korean relative clauses, it should be recognized that Korean relative clauses can receive various interpretations. The fact that the head noun is normally interpreted as an obligatory argument of the verb in a relative clause does not always apply to Korean. If it is more natural for a particular head−noun to be interpreted as a non−argument of the verb in the relative clause, a pragmatically plausible interpretation can be preferred to a syntactically motivated interpretation in Korean.

6.2. Tense of relative clauses

The tense of relative clauses in Korean is indicated by the adnominal ending of the verb in the relative clause. The interpretation of a head-noun can be varied depending on the tense of relative clauses. Consider the following examples:

(49) a. [tambay-lul   sa-n]   canton

cigarette-Acc buy-Rel(Past) change

'The change that left over after buying cigarettes'[8]

b. [tambay-lul   sa-nun/l]   canton

cigarette-Acc buy-Rel(Pres/Fut)   change

'The change that will be/is used to buy cigarettes'

Depending on the tense of the verb, the head-noun *canton* 'change' can indicate different referents, i.e. the change after the purchase and the change that is/will be used for the purchase.

6.3. Interpretation depending on adjunct elements

The grammaticality of the relative clause can be changed depending on

---

8   An anonymous reviewer pointed out that 'the change' in this example could also be interpreted as 'the change that was used to buy cigarettes'.

whether or not an additional adjunct is added or not. In this case, the added element helps to identify grammatical roles of the head-noun. Consider the following examples:

(50) a. *Yumi-ka   mek-un   salam

　　　　Nom   eat-Rel   person

　　　'*The person who Yumi ate'

　　b. Yumi-ka   hamkkey   mek-un   salam

　　　　Nom   together   eat-Rel   person

　　　'The person with whom Yumi ate'

(50a) cannot be accepted as a natural sentence,[9] but it becomes much more natural when an adverb *hamkkey* 'together' is added as in (50b). Adverbs such as *kathi* 'together' or *hamkkey* 'together' play a role in iden-tifying the grammatical role of the comitative particle, which is omitted in the formation of relative clauses. The same applies to the following examples:

(51) a. *Yongsu-ka   san-ey　　ka-n   Suni

　　　　Nom   mountain-Loc   go-Rel

　　　'*Suni who Yongsu went to the mountain'

9　An anonymous reviewer pointed out that if Yumi was a cannibal (or in a situation where she was bound to eat a person), this example could be acceptable. I agree with the reviewer but we consider only the pragmatic context at the level of common sense.

b. Yongsu-ka   kathi/hamkkey san-ey   ka-n Suni

    Nom   together   mountain-Loc go-Rel

   'Suni with whom Yongsu wnet to the mountain'

The comitative NP in (51a) cannot become a head-noun as already pointed out in (6) above, but if an adverb *kathi* or *hamkkey* 'together' is inserted, (51b) can be acceptable.

6.4. Interpretation based on context

The interpretation of the same relative clause can vary depending on the contextual meaning of the main clause. Consider the following examples:

(52) a. na-nun chengchepcang-ul   ponay-n   chinkwu-tul-hanthey

     I-Top wedding.invitation-Acc send-Rel   friend-PL-Dat

     chwukuykum-ul ponay-ess-ta.

     gift money-Acc   send-Past-Dec

     "I sent gift money to friends who sent me a wedding invitation.'

   b. na-nun chengchepcang-ul ponay-n chinkwu-tul-hanthey

     I-Top wedding.invitation-Acc send-Rel   friend-PL-Dat

     hwakinmeyil-to hamkkey ponay-ess-ta.

     confirmation mail-too together send-Past-Dec

     'I sent confirmation mails as well to friends to whom I sent a wedding

     invitation.'

(52) is an example in which the interpretation of relative clauses can be varied according to the contextual meaning of the following main clause. On the other hand, it is also possible that the interpretation of the relative clause can be changed according to the contextual meaning of the preceding sentence. Consider the following example.

(53) manna-kilo ha-n   yeca-nun   cip-ulo   ka-peli-ess-ta.

meet-arrange.to-Rel   woman-Top home-Loc go-Aux-Past-Dec

'The woman (with whom) (I) have arranged to meet has gone home.'

When (53) stands alone, the preferred interpretation would be 'the woman (with whom) I (speaker) have arranged to meet'. However, interpretation may be changed if the following context is given:

(54) namca-wa yeca-ka   manna-kilo ha-ess-ciman,   sikan-i

man-and woman-Nom   meet-arrange.to-Past-but,   time-Nom

cina-to   sangtaypang-un nathanaci-anh-ass-ta.

pass-even though counterpart-Top show.up-Neg-Past-Dec

Manna-kilo ha-n   yeca-nun   cip-ulo   ka-peli-ess-ta.

meet-arrange.to-Rel girl-Top   home-Loc go-Aux-Past-Dec

'The man and woman arranged to meet, but the man did not show up

as time passed.

The woman (who) arranged to meet (him) has gone home.'

In this case, the woman is the agent of the meeting and she is the subject who meets the man. The reason for this diverse interpretation is that Korean does not need to specify all the arguments in a sentence, unlike English. We therefore do not have to interpret the head nouns of the relative clauses as obligatory arguments of the verb. Furthermore, in Korean, adjuncts that are not arguments in sentences can become head nouns of relative clauses, therefore various interpretations are possible. This implies that Korean relative clauses are not fully explained based on syntactic information alone and requires pragmatic information, including higher level of extra-linguistic knowledge.

7. Conclusion

Prior studies on relative clauses have focused primarily on the morphology and syntactic nature of the sentence. However, as we have seen so far, various pragmatic factors and extra-linguistic knowledge play important roles in the formation and interpretation of Korean relative clauses. Therefore, further research is needed on these peculiarities.

Comrie(1998, 2002) proposed that relative clauses in East Asian languages should be treated as attributive clauses rather than European-type relative clauses, based on the observation that relativizability is constrained not by grammatical relations but by semantic and pragmatic factors in these languages. With special reference to Japanese, Matsumoto(1990, 1997) offered an explanation based on semantic and pragmatic – rather than syntactic – conditions to determine the availability of noun-modifying clauses in Japanese. Based on her work, Comrie(1996, 1998, 2002) proposed a new typology that distinguishes Japanese and other Asian languages with similar properties from European-type languages. He proposed that noun-modifying clauses in many Asian languages (e.g. Chinese, Japanese and Korean) are qualitatively different from those in European languages because these Asian languages do not have relative clauses with a gap but, rather, have attributive clauses, which involve simply attaching modifying clauses to the head noun.

In this respect, Fox and Thompson's(1990a, 1990b) claim provides a very interesting implication. They have argued that strict syntactic argument constraints are required in N-Rel type languages while semantic-pragmatic interpretations are required in Rel-N type languages. The reason for the differences can be attributed to the difference in information processing between the N-Rel type and the Rel-N type language. In the N-Rel type language, the head noun comes before the relative clause, so it is followed by the explanation of the head noun. Thus, the speaker of the N-Rel type language is required to provide the listener with information about the head noun for the information processing. The information include grammatical information such as case, gender, and number of the head noun, which is provided through relative pronouns. The listener's expectation for syntactic information can be met through this process(Rumelhart 1977). On the other hand, in the Rel-N type language, the information about the head noun is presented properly in a preceding relative clause, and the listener interprets the most appropriate candidate from the given context as the appropriate head noun. At the same time, the listener can appropriately deduce the syntactic relationship between the preceding verb in relative clauses and the following head noun based on this pragmatic information rather than syntactic information, so that there is room for various pragmatic information to intervene.

This paper thus demonstrates that interpretation of Korean relative clauses depends on context and pragmatic factors. Pragmatic factors and extra-linguistic knowledge play important roles in acceptability judgments and therefore those factors should be considered in the interpretation of Korean relative clauses. This paper has convincingly proven the significant role played by pragmatic factors in the interpretation of relative clauses in Korean.

References

Cha, Jong-Yul (2005), *Constraints on Clausal Complex Noun Phrases in Korean with Focus on the Gapless Relative Clause Construction*, Doctoral dissertation, University of Illinois at Urbana-Champaign.

Chae, Hee-Rak (2012), "*Hankwuk.e ey kwayen kwankyecel i concayhanunka: pwunsacel pwunsek* (Are There Relative Clauses in Korean?: A Participle Clause Analysis)," Korean Journal of Linguistics 37(4), 1043-1064.

Comrie, B. (1996), The unity of noun-modifying clauses in Asian languages. In *Proceedings of the 4th International Symposium on Pan-Asiatic Linguistics*: 1077-1088. Salaya, Thailand: Institute of Language and Culture for Rural Development, Mahidol University of Salaya.

Comrie, B. (1998), Attributive clauses in Asian languages: Towards an areal typology. In W. Boeder, C. Schroeder, K. H. Wagner, & W. Wildgen (Eds.), *Sprache in Raum und Zeit: In memoriam Johannes Bechert, Band*, 2, 51-60. Tuebingen: Gunter Narr.

Comrie, B. (2002), Typology and language acquisition: The case of relative clauses. In A. Giacalone Ramat (Ed.), *Typology and second language acquisition*, 19-37. Berlin: Mouton de Gruyter.

Fox, B. and S. Thompson. (1990a), A Discourse Explanation of the Grammar of Relative Clauses in English Conversation. *Language* 66, 297-316.

Fox, B. and S. Thompson. (1990b), On Formulating Reference: An Interactional Approach to Relative Clauses in English Conversation. *Papers in Pragmatics* 4, 183-95.

Keenan, E.L. and Comrie, B. (1977), "Noun Phrase Accessibility and Universal Grammar." *Linguistic Inquiry*: 8(1), 63-99.

Kim, Min-gook. (2010), Haykemyengsa uy kwankyehwa cenlyak ey tayhan yenkwu. (A Study on the restriction of relativization of head noun) *Hankwuk ehak* (Korean Linguistics) 47, 131-162.

Kuno, S. (1973), *The structure of the Japanese Language*, Cambridge MA: MIT Press.

Lee, Chungmin. and Jeong-Shik Lee. (2012), Gap in "Gapless" Relative Clauses in Korean and Other Asian Languages. *UCLA Working Papers in Linguistics, Theories of Everything* Vol. 17, Article 25, 204-214.

Lee, Hongbae. (1975), 'Kuwke uy kwankyecelhwa ey tayhaye (On Korean relativization)', Language Research 11(2), 289-300.

Lee, Jieun. (2017a), Relativization in Korean: Formal Limitations and Functional Solutions. PhD thesis. University of Otago, New Zealand.

Lee, Jieun. (2017b), (In)compatibility between relative clauses and topic constructions. *Hyengthaylon* (Morphology) 19(2), 198-217.

Matsumoto, Y. (1988), Semantic and pragmatics of noun-modifying constructions in Japanese. *Proceedings of the Annual Meeting of the Berkeley Linguistics Society*, 14, 166-175.

Matsumoto, Y. (1989), Japanese style noun modification ⋯ in English. *BLS* 15, 226-37.

Matsumoto, Y. (1990), The role of pragmatics in Japanese relative clause constructions. *Lingua* 82, 111-29.

Matsumoto, Y. (1996), "Interaction of Factors in Construal: Japanese Relative Clauses". In Shibatani, Masayoshi and Thompson, S.A., eds. 1996: *Grammatical Constructions: their form and meaning*. Oxford: Clarendon Press.

Matsumoto, Y. (1997), *Noun-modifying constructions in Japanese: A frame-semantic approach*, Amsterdam: Benjamins.

Mun, Suk-Yeong. (2012), *Yuhyenglon cek kwancem eyse pon hankwuk.e kwankyecel uy myech muncey* (A study on Korean relative clauses in typological perspectives) Gaesin Emun Yenkwu. Vol. 35, 31-68. Gaesin Language and Literature Society: Korea.

Na, Younghee. (1986), *Syntactic and semantic interaction in Korean: theme, topic, and relative clauses*, Unpublished PhD dissertation. University of Chicago.

Pustejovsky, James. (1995), *The Generative Lexicon*, MIT Press. Cambridge, MA.

Pustejovsky, James. (2005), *Meaning in Context: Mechanisms of Selection in*

Language, MIT Press, Cambridge, MA.

Rumelhart, David E. (1977), *Introduction to Human Information Processing*, New York: John Wiley & Sons, Inc.

Shin, Hyophil. (1994), *Hankwuk.e kwankye kwumun uy thongsa wa uymi kwuco* (The Syntax and semantics of Korean relative clause constructions), PhD dissertation, Seoul National University. Seoul.

Song, J. (1991), Korean relative clause constructions: Conspiracy and pragmatics. *Australian Journal of Linguistics*, 11(2), 195–220.

Tagashira, Y. (1972), Relative Clauses in Korean. In: Peranteau, P.M., Levi, J.N. and Phares, G.C. (eds.) The Chicago which hunt: Papers from the relative clause festival, Chicago: Chicago Linguistic Society, 215–229.

Yang, Dong-Whee (1975), Topicalization and relativization in Korean, Ann Arbor, MI: University Microfilms International.

Yeom, Jae-il (2015), Gapless Adnominal Clauses in Korean and their Interpretations. *Language Research* 51(3), 597–627.

Yeom, Jae-il. (2017), Coerced Relative Clauses in Korean. *Language Research*, 53(2), 287–320.

Yeon, Jaehoon (2003), *Korean Grammatical Constructions: Their Form and Meaning*. London: Saffron books.

Yeon, Jaehoon. (2012), *Yuhyenglon cek kwancem uy hankwuk.e kwankyecel yenkwu* (A functional-typological study on Korean relative clauses). Journal of Korean Linguistics. 63, 413–457.

화용적 원리의 신경기반 연구

김지영

1. 서론

노벨상 수상자인 생리의학자 Gerald Edelman(1992)은 "비비원숭이를 이해할 줄 아는 사람이 존 로크보다 훨씬 더 형이상학에 공헌하게 될 것"이라는 찰스 다윈의 예견을 소개하며, 뇌의 구조나 작용과 무관하게 이루어지는 형이상학적 연구에 대해 신랄하게 비판하였고, 신경학자 Antonio Damasio 또한 Descartes' Error(2000)에서 신경과학 분야의 여러 사례들을 통해 몸과 마음이 분리된 것이 아님을 역설하였다.

실제로 최근 수십 년간 신경과학의 눈부신 발전은 인간의 정신활동 중 그 어떤 것도 신경회로에 연결되지 않은 것이 없다는 것을 밝혀내고 있고, 이에 따라 철학, 심리학, 언어학 등에서도 특정 정신활동의 신경학적 기반을 밝혀내는 데 많은 노력을 기울이고 있다. 신경화용론 분야에서는 간접 화행이나 비유적 표현을 포함한 화용적 발화의 이해에 동원되는 뇌의 영역을 찾거나 뇌의 손상으로 인해 화용적 능력에 어떤 장애가 생기는지 등을 연구하고 있다.

그런데 화용론은 축어적 의미와는 다른 화자의 의미가 어떻게 발생하는 지를 탐구하는 분야로서, 여러 이론에서 제안하는 화용적 원리는 간접 화행, 은유 등 다양한 형태의 화자의 의미가 발생하는 근거를 제시하는 것을 목적으로 하고 있다. 따라서 앞서 언급한 신경과학의 발견과 화용론 이론을 함께 고려하면, 축어적 의미가 아닌 화용적 의미를 이해하기 위하여 우리의 인지에는 일종의 화용적 원리가 작동할 것이고, 이러한 원리의 작동에는 뇌의 특정 부위나 영역의 활성화가 필수적으로 수반될 것이라는 뜻이 된다. 하지만 지금까지의 신경화용론 연구 중 그 어디에서도 특정 현상을 넘어선 일반적인 화용적 원리 자체의 신경 상관물을 발견하고자 하는 시도는 찾을 수 없다. 가령 Jang, Yoon, Lee, Park, Kim, Ko, and Park(2013)은 관련성 함축 의미(relevance implicature)의 이해과정에 대한 뇌영상 연구를 실시하여, 암시성(implicitness)의 정도가 높을 때와 낮을 때의 뇌의 활성 패턴이 다르다는 결과를 내놓았는데, 그들은 관련성 함축의미가 관련성의 격률(Maxim of Relevance)을 어김으로써 생성되는 반면, 반어나 은유는 질의 격률(Maxim of Quality)을 어김으로써 생성되는 것이기 때문에 서로 다른 인지적 초점과 발생과정, 그리고 동일하지 않은 신경기반을 바탕으로 한다고 보았다. 즉 Jang et al.(2013)은 함축의미, 반어, 은유 등 개별 현상을 이해할 때 동원되는 신경 기반이 어떻게 다른지에 초점을 맞추고 있다는 것을 알 수 있는데, 본고에서 초점을 맞추고자 하는 것은 아무리 다른 개별 현상이라 하더라도 화용적 원리는 정의상 화용적 의미를 해석할 때 언제나 작동하는 것이기 때문에 어떤 현상을 이해할 때에라도 화용적 원리에 해당하는 신경 상관물은 활성 화될 것이라는 점이다.

따라서 본고는 그간 신경화용론적 연구에서 화용적 이해에 동원되는 것으로 보고된 다양한 뇌의 부위에는 화용적 원리의 작동에 해당하는 부위가 포함되어 있을 것으로 상정하고 그중 어떤 것이 화용적 원리에 해당되는지를 추정해보는 것을 목적으로 하고 있다. 만약 우리가 개별적인 현상을 이해하는 데 동원되는 뇌 부위를 찾는 데에 그치지 않고 그 현상의 이해를 가능하게 하는 원리의 신경 부위 혹은 회로를 찾을 수 있다면 우리가 어떻게 화용적 현상을 이해할 수 있는지를 더 깊이 통찰할 수 있을 것이다.

연구의 개요에 앞서 아래 (1)의 대화를 통해 화용론 이론이 작동하는 방식에 대하여 간략히 살펴보자.

(1) A: 지금 몇 시지?

B: 응? 이제 뭐 좀 먹을까?

A: 그러자.

1970년대 이래 화용론적 연구를 선도해 온 Grice(1975)의 협동의 원리(Cooperative Principle)와 네 가지 격률(Maxims of conversation)은 의사소통에서 추론의 발생과 함축의미 복원의 바탕이 된다. (1)에서 B가 A의 물음에 답하는 대신 다른 질문을 하는 인지적 과정을 이 이론에 따라 해석하면, B는 A가 대화의 목적에 맞게 기여하여 협동의 원리를 준수할 뿐 아니라 관계의 격률(Maxim of relevance)을 지킬 것으로 상정하고 있으며 그러할 경우 A의 발화 "지금 몇 시지?"의 해석은 '식사시간, 출발이나 도착시간, 일의 시작이나 끝맺음 시간, 단순 호기심' 등 시간을 궁금해 하는 여러 일반적 이유 중 하나일 것이라고 상정할 수 있다. 이와 더불어 B는 발화의 상황적 맥락(예: 정오를 지난 시간)과 화자 A에 대한 지식(예: 정오 즈음에 점심식사를 함)을 고려하여 '식사시간이 다 되었는지 묻고 있다'는 함축의미를 추론해냈을 것이다. 자신의 추론결과를 바탕으로 B는 '이제 뭐 좀 먹을까?'라는 제안을 하였으며

A의 '그러자'는 대답으로 자신의 추론이 맞았음을 확인할 수 있을 것이다.

다른 한편 1990년대 이후 화용론에 대한 인지적, 심리학적 연구의 꽃을 피운 Sperber and Wilson(1986)의 적합성원리(Relevance principle)에서는 협동의 원리가 아닌 적합성에 대한 추구가 의사소통을 이끄는 인간 인지의 기본 원리라고 주장한다. 적합성은 입력된 정보를 처리하는 노력이 덜 들수록, 그리고 인지적 효과가 더 클수록 그 정도가 더 커지는 인지적 효율성의 다른 이름이다. 적합성원리의 설명을 따라 (1)을 분석해보면, B는 우선 '의미보충(semantic enrichment)'을 통해 화자 A의 표현에서 논리형식을 발전시킨 후 'A는 현재의 시간을 묻고 있다'는 외축의미(explicature)를 복원해낸다. 이 외축의미가 B에게서 최대의 인지적 효과, 즉 최적의 적합성을 얻는 방법은 해당 발화의 시간과 장소가 상호현시화(mutually manifest)된 상태에서 백과사전적 지식인 시간을 궁금해 할 만한 용건들을 구정보로 하여 'A는 식사시간이 되었는지를 묻고 있다'는 맥락적 함축(contextual implication)을 얻어내는 것이다. 비록 이 과정은 단순히 "12시 반이야"와 같이 답하는 것보다 훨씬 더 많은 처리노력을 들이겠지만 그 노력에 대해 충분히 보상받을 수 있을 만큼 더 큰 효과를 얻을 수 있다. 그리고 이러한 처리 과정을 이끄는 것이 바로 Sperber and Wilson(1986)이 제안하는 인간의 보편적 인지 능력인 적합성 원리인 것이다.

이와 같이 화용론 이론의 목적은 입력된 언어적 기호를 물리적, 정신적 맥락 속에서 해석함으로써 화자의 의도에 맞게 해석하도록 이끄는 인지적 원리를 설명하고자 하는 것이다. 이 원리들은 화자가 알맞은 표현을 생산하는 과정이나 청자가 해석하는 과정에서 언제나 지킬 것으로 예상되는 것이며 더 나아가 인간 인지의 기본 자질이다. 따라서 (1)의 A와 B가 의식하든 의식하지 못하든 화용적 의미를 처리할 때 이 원리들은 언제나 작동하고 있다는 뜻이다. 그렇다면 이러한 화용적 원리가 작동할 때는 뇌의 어느 부위가 활성화되는 것일까?

다음 2절에서는 신경화용론 연구를 개괄하고, 3절에서는 화용적 발화의 이해나 생산에 특정적으로 활성화된다고 발표된 신경화용론적 결과들을 정리하여 소개한다. 4절에서는 이 결과들을 토대로 몇몇 서로 다른 화용적 발화에서 활성화가 가능한 영역들을 취합하고, 5절에서는 이 중 화용적 원리로 삼을 만한 영역에 대한 가설을 수립한 후 각각의 타당성을 논하는 과정에서 과연 화용적 원리에 대한 특정 신경 상관물이 존재하는지에 대해 의문을 제기할 것이다.

2. 신경화용론 연구의 개요

인간 두뇌의 피질(cortex)에서 일차 감각 및 운동을 담당하는 영역은 해당 기능과 영역을 일대일로 대응하는 것이 가능할 정도로 피질의 기능적 전문성이 명백히 드러났다.[1] 또한 언어의 조음 및 통사, 의미 등 언어의 형식적 기능에 대해서는 1860년대 Paul Broca나 Carl Wernicke 등이 실어증 환자의 사후 뇌 해부를 통해 좌반구의 전두엽과 측두엽의 일정 부위에서 병소(lesion)를 발견하면서 그 부위를 특정하는 것이 어느 정도 가능하게 되었다. 하지만 그로부터 한 세기가 지나서 시작된 화용적 기능과 뇌의 기제에 대한 연구는 화용적 현상의 광범위하고 복잡한 성격으로 인해 뇌의 일정 부위가

---

1   두뇌의 중심구(central sulcus)를 경계로 앞뒤로 위치한 운동 영역과 체감각 영역은 해당 기능에 따라 정교한 피질 지도가 완성되어, 두뇌에 존재하는 극미(極微)의 인간이라는 뜻의 'homunculus'라는 명칭이 붙어 있다.

일정한 화용적 기능을 담당한다고 특정하기보다는 특정 화용적 현상에 대해 반응하는 뇌의 영역을 찾는 일을 하고 있다.

뇌 기능과 언어의 화용적 수행에 대한 관심은 우반구 손상(right hemisphere damage) 환자들이 좌반구 손상으로 인한 실어증과는 다른 문제로 인해 미묘한 의사소통적 장애를 겪는다는 점에 주목하면서 비롯되었다(Critchley 1962, Eisenson 1962).[2] 이후 Winner and Gardner(1977)는 우반구 손상 환자들에게 가령 'He had a heavy heart'라는 문장에 어울리는 그림을 고르게 했을 때 '울고 있는 사람'이 아닌 '크기가 큰 심장을 들고 있는 사람'의 그림을 고르는 등 통제집단에 비해 문장을 축어적으로 해석하는 비율이 현저히 높다고 보고하였고, Delis, Wapner, Gardner, and Moses(1983)는 한 문단에 속하는 문장들을 순서대로 배열하는 과제에서 우반구 손상 환자들이 통제집단에 비해 현격히 낮은 수행능력을 보인다고 보고하였다. 또한 Kaplan, Brownell, Jacobs, and Gardner(1990)는 우반구 손상 환자들이 주어진 상황에 대한 축어적 설명을 이해하는 데는 별 문제가 없으나, 화용적인 간접적 설명을 이해하는 데는 상당한 어려움을 보인다는 결과를 제시하였다. 이러한 일련의 연구들은 우반구 손상 환자들이 겪는 문제가 언어의 축어적 이해보다는 화자의 의도 파악을 전제로 하는 화용적 이해에 국한되는 경향이 있으므로 언어의 화용적 기능이 우반구의 기능에서 비롯되었을 것이라는 가설에 힘을 싣는 결과를 낳았다.

하지만 이 가설은 1990년대 기능적 뇌 영상 기술(functional neuroimaging)의[3] 등장과 발전으로 힘을 잃게 되었고, 현재는 양반구의 여러 중심 지역이

---

2   Joanette and Goulet(1994:3)에서 인용함.

3   신경화용론에서 사용되는 뇌 영상 기술에는 양전자 방출 단층 촬영술(positron emission tomography, PET), 기능성 자기공명 영상술(functional magnetic resonanace imaging,

상호작용하면서 화용적 처리에 기여하고 있음이 밝혀지고 있다(Bambini and Bara 2012). 예를 들어, Hagoort and van Berkum(2007)은 ERP 결과를 통해 문장, 맥락, 세상지식, 제스처 등 여러 원천의 정보가 입력 즉시 통합된다는 것을 보임으로써 문장 수준의 의미 처리와 화용적 의미 처리가 두 단계가 아닌 한 단계로 이루어진다고 주장하였는데, 이 통합 과정에서 좌반구에 위치한 하전두회(left inferior frontal gyrus, lIFG)가 주된 역할을 한다는 것을 포착하였다. 또한 Bara and Ciaramidaro(2010)는 상대방을 고려해야 하는 '의사소통적 의도'의 표상에 내전전두피질(medial prefrontal cortex, mPFC), 측두두정경계(temporo-pariental juncture, TPJ), 쐐기앞소엽(precuneus) 등 좌, 우 양반구의 여러 지역이 동원된다는 결과를 내놓음으로써 화용적 언어 처리가 우반구만이 아닌 좌, 우 양반구의 기여로 이루어진다는 것이 밝혀지고 있는 것이다.

다른 한편 인간의 행동과 두뇌와의 관계에 대한 연구는 일반인뿐 아니라 다양한 뇌 손상 환자를 대상으로 진행되는 경우가 많은데 그 이유는 뇌의 특정 부위의 손상이 일정한 인지 능력의 손실로 이어지기 때문에 그 손상된

---

fMRI), 사건관련 전위(event-related potential, ERP), 뇌자도(magnetoencephalography, MEG) 등이 있는데, 각 기술의 장, 단점을 비교하면 다음과 같다. PET와 fMRI는 뇌의 부위가 활성화되어 산소를 소모할 경우 일어나는 신경의 활성을 이용하여 간접적으로 뇌의 활동을 측정하는 방식으로, PET는 방사성 동위원소를 주입하여 양전자 방출을 촬영하기 때문에 방사선 노출에 대한 규정으로 데이터를 손쉽게 얻을 수 없는 데 반해, 방사선 노출에 대한 염려 없이 혈액의 산화도를 측정하는 fMRI는 PET보다 공간적, 시간적 해상도도 더 뛰어나 인지신경과학에서 사용하는 보편적인 도구이다. 하지만 fMRI는 인지 활동을 실시간 기록할 수 없는 한계가 있다. 다른 한편 ERP는 두피에 전극을 설치하여 천 분의 몇 초 단위로(milliseconds) 뇌의 전기 활동을 측정하므로 fMRI보다 시간적 해상도에서 효과가 뛰어나지만 정확히 어느 부위에서 일어난 활동인지 특정하기 어렵다. 마지막으로 MEG는 뇌 세포의 자기신호를 측정하는 방법으로 시간해상도도 뛰어나고 활성 세포의 위치도 국소화할 수 있으나 장비의 높은 가격으로 보급도가 낮다는 단점이 있다.

부위가 담당하는 기능이 무엇이었는지를 역으로 찾아내는 것이 용이하기 때문이다. 따라서 화용적 언어 사용에 동원되는 뇌 영역을 찾는 연구 또한 위에 언급한 우반구 손상뿐 아니라 자폐증(autism)이나 외상성 뇌손상(traumatic brain injury) 환자 등 다양한 병리 집단을 대상으로 실시되고 있다. 언어사용 능력과 관련하여 이들이 보이는 공통점에는 언어의 통사와 의미 체계는 대체로 유지하지만 화자의 의도를 이해하지 못하는 어려움을 겪는다거나 문장 단위의 이해에는 문제가 없지만 전체 이야기의 주제는 파악하지 못한다는 점, 표현의 축어적 이해에는 별 어려움이 없지만 은유, 반어, 농담 등은 잘 이해하지 못한다는 점, 그리고 얼굴에 드러난 감정과 말의 운율을 파악하지 못한다는 점 등 소위 화용적 능력에 대해 비슷한 유형의 장애를 보인다는 점이다.

다음 절에서는 이를 포함한 다양한 연구를 통해 밝혀진, 여러 화용적 현상에 동원되는 구체적인 뇌 영역과 그 영역의 알려진 기능 등을 살펴볼 것이다.

3. 화용적 현상과 뇌 영역

3.1. 마음이론 기제

'마음이론(theory of mind)'이라는 용어는 Premack and Woodruff(1978)가 고안한 것으로,[4] 한 개인이 목적, 의도, 믿음 등의 정신적 상태(mental states)

---

4 Premack and Woodruff(1978)는 정신적 상태가 직접적으로 관찰 가능한 것이 아니기 때문에 마음/정신(mind)에 대한 '이론(theory)'이라는 용어를 사용하였다.

가 자기 자신이나 다른 사람에게 있다고 추론할 수 있는 능력을 뜻하며, 인간은 이 능력을 자신과 타인의 행동을 이해하고 예측하기 위해 사용하는 것으로 보인다. 따라서 마음이론 기제는 화용적 언어 사용을 근본적으로 가능하게 할 뿐 아니라 화용적 능력의 손상을 야기한다고 지목되는 신경기제 중 가장 중요하게 다뤄지고 있다.[5]

마음이론 기제의 뇌 영역에는 내전전두피질(mPFC), 측두두정경계(TPJ), 상측두구(superior temporal sulcus, STS), 하측두회(inferior temporal gyrus, ITG), 편도(amygdala)(Kandel, Schwartz, Jessell, Siegelbaum, and Hudspeth 2013: Part IV), 그리고 전인접대상피질(anterior paracingulate cortex, aPCC)과 측두극(temporal poles, TP)(Gallagher and Frith 2003) 등이 포함된다고 알려져 있다(각 부위의 뇌에서의 위치에 대하여 그림 1을 참조하시오).

---

5   화용적 언어의 손상을 야기하는 신경기제에는 마음이론 외에 '약한 중앙적 결속성(weak central coherence)'과 '실행기능(executive function)'이 있다. 약한 중앙적 결속성 가설은 자폐증 환자들이 지엽적 처리에는 능하나 전체 그림을 보지 못한다는 것을 발견한 후 제안되었고, 이 측면이 언어에 적용되면 어떤 진술의 참, 거짓은 알 수 있으나 맥락 내에서는 그 의미를 설명할 수 없는 현상으로 나타난다. 하지만 이 가설은 윌리엄스 증후군 환자들이 자폐증의 증상과 마찬가지로 전체 그림은 보지 못하지만 화용적 언어 사용에는 아주 능하다는 점에서 문제가 제기된다. 한편, 실행기능은 다양한 환경에서 자신의 계획에 맞게 행동을 조정하는 일군의 인지적 처리과정을 말한다. 전두엽의 주요 기능인 이 실행기능에는 주의 집중, 작업기억, 억제력, 유연성 등의 기능이 포함되며, 이 기능들 중 여럿이 동시에 작동하여 언어이해를 비롯한 고차원적 추론이 가능해진다. 그런데 뇌 손상 환자들 중 일반적 추론은 가능하나 대인관계 속에서의 사회적 추론에만 선택적으로 문제가 있는 경우에는 실행기능 가설이 성립하기 어렵다(Martin and McDonald(2003)의 논의를 요약함).

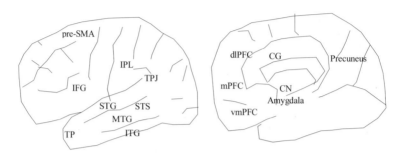

[그림 1] 각 부위의 뇌에서의 위치
(좌뇌의 외부면(좌측 그림)과 뇌의 시상면(우측 그림))

(pre-SMA(전부운동영역), IFG(하전두회), IPL(하두정엽), TPJ(측두두정경계),
TP(측두극), STG(상측두회), MTG(중측두회), ITG(하측두회), STS(상측두구),
mPFC(내전전두피질), dlPFC(배외전전두피질), vmPFC(복내전전두피질), CG(Cingulate
gyrus, 대상회), Precuneus(쐐기앞소엽), CN(꼬리핵), Amygdala(편도))

이중 내전전두피질(mPFC)은 생각을 스스로 모니터링하며, 자신에게 유리
한 판단을 내리고, 실행을 통제하는 지역이다(Euston, Gruber, and McNaughton
2012). 측두두정경계(TPJ)는 측두엽(기억의 주요 장소), 두정엽(체감각 담당), 후
두엽(시각 담당), 변연계(감정, 기억 담당) 등으로부터 정보가 모이는 곳으로
자신과 타인을 구별하여 타인의 정신적 상태를 파악할 수 있도록 도와준다
(Quesque and Brass 2019). 또한 상측두구(STS)는 생물학적 움직임에 대해 반
응하며, 상대방 행동의 의도를 인지하는 데 중요한 역할을 하고(Pelphrey,
Morris, and McCarthy 2004), 하측두회(ITG)는 얼굴을 인식하여 비언어적 의사소
통을 지원한다(Conway 2018). 환경으로부터의 위험을 알리는 편도(amygdala)는
마음이론의 발달에 영향을 주는 것으로 알려졌다(Shaw, Lawrence, Radbourne,
Bramham, Polkey, and David 2004). 또한 전인접대상피질(aPCC)은 실제와 분리
된 정신적 상태를 표상하는 능력을 뒷받침하고, 측두극(TP)은 개인의 의미

적, 일화적 기억(semantic and episodic memories)의 저장소로서 상대방의 현재 행동을 예측하는 데 도움을 준다(Gallagher and Frith 2003).

Baron-Cohen, Leslie, and Frith(1985)는 '틀린 믿음 과제(false belief tasks)'[6] 실험을 통해 자폐아동들의 인지적 손실이 마음이론 능력의 장애로 인한 것임을 밝혔고, 다른 병리집단, 예를 들어 우반구 손상 환자들의 연구에서도 간접 요청 같은 언어의 화용적 이해의 문제를 마음이론과 연관 짓고 있다 (Champagne-Lavau and Joanette 2009).

3.2. 간접 요청의 신경 기제

화용적 언어 사용의 가장 대표적인 현상은 화행으로, 신경화용론에서도 간접 요청 등 화행에 대한 연구가 활발히 이루어지고 있다. 가령 van Ackeren, Casasanto, Bekkering, Hagoort, and Rueschemeyer(2012)는 'It's hot in here. (여기가 덥네요)'라는 문장이 사막의 날씨를 묘사하는 진술문(statement)으로 쓰일 때보다 '문을 열어달라'는 간접 요청으로 쓰일 때 활성을 보이는 부위를 찾고자 하였는데, 가장 큰 활성을 보이는 곳은 위에 언급한 마음이론 영역이고, 이와 함께 양반구의 하두정엽(inferior parietal lobe, IPL)과 전부운동

---

6   Wimmer and Perner(1983)의 틀린 믿음 과제(false belief tasks)를 사용한 Baron-Cohen et al.(1985)의 실험은 다음과 같이 진행되었다. Sally와 Anne이라는 이름의 인형이 두 개 있다. → 처음에 참가 아동들에게 인형의 이름을 알고 있는지 확인한다(이름 대기 질문). → Sally가 자신의 바구니에 구슬을 하나 집어넣은 후 그 자리에서 나간다. → Anne이 그 구슬을 자신의 상자로 옮겨 넣고 뚜껑을 덮는다. → 이제 Sally가 돌아왔다. → 실험 진행자가 아동들에게 "Sally는 구슬을 찾으러 어디를 볼까요?"라고 묻는다(믿음 질문). → 참가 아동이 구슬의 원래 위치를 가리키면 인형 Sally의 현재의 '틀린 믿음'을 이해하는 것이므로 '믿음 질문'을 통과한다. → 하지만 구슬의 현재 위치를 가리키면 인형 Sally의 믿음을 고려하지 못한 것이기 때문에 통과하지 못한다.

영역(pre-supplementary motor area, pre-SMA)도 크게 활성화된다는 것을 관찰였는데, 이는 화행을 이해하는 데는 운동의 심상과 계획, 통제, 실수 예상 등을 담당하는 영역 역시 동원된다는 뜻으로 해석된다(각 부위의 뇌에서의 위치에 대하여 그림 1을 참조하시오).

3.3. 은유의 신경 기제

비축어적 표현인 은유(metaphor)의 이해는 대표적인 화용적 현상의 하나로 꼽히는데, 이러한 은유의 신경적 기반에 대한 연구는 우반구의 활성이 포함되느냐 마느냐에 대한 논쟁으로 요약될 수 있는데, Bottini, Corcoran, Sterzi, Paulesu, Schenone, Scarpa, Frackowiak, and Frith(1994)는 두뇌에 이상이 없는 참가자들의 은유 해석에서 축어적 문장의 해석에 동원되는 좌우반구의 여러 지역 외에도 우반구의 전전두 피질(right prefrontal cortex, rPFC), 쐐기앞소엽(precuneus), 중측두회(middle temporal gyrus, MTG) 등이 특별한 역할을 한다고 보고하였다.[7] 하지만 Rapp, Leube, Erb, Grodd, and Kircher (2004)는 Bottini et al.의 연구에서 사용한 은유 표현에는 'The policeman who didn't give straight answers was jumping ditches.(정직한 대답을 하지 않은 그 경찰관은 도랑 위를 뛰어가고 있었다)'와 같이 지나치게 복잡한 문장을 사용하였기 때문에 이러한 결과가 나온 것이라고 지적하고, 'The alarm clock is a torturer.(알람시계는 고문기계다)'와 같이 간단한 문장을 사용한 자신들의 연구에서는 좌하전두회(lIFG)와 좌중/하측두회(left middle and inferior

---

7   Bottini et al.(1994)은 우전전두피질(rPFC)과 쐐기앞소엽(precuneus)은 장기기억에서 단어의 의미를 인출하는 역할을, 중측두회(MTG)는 복잡한 의미적 판단을 내리는 역할을 한다고 보았다.

temporal gyri, lMTG/lITG)에서 가장 강력한 신호의 변화를 보여, 은유 이해에 우반구의 개입이 필수적이지도 않고 특정적이지도 않다고 주장하였다.[8] 하지만 Schmidt and Seger(2009)는 Rapp et al.(2004)의 결과와 반대로 우반구도 분명히 개입한다는 결과를 내놓았다. 그들은 상투적인 은유 표현의 해석에는 주로 좌반구의 전통적인 언어영역인 브로카(좌하전두회, lIFG) 및 베르니케 영역(좌상측두회, left superior temporal gyrus, lSTG)과 의미처리를 위한 측두극(TP) 등이 활성화되었지만, 더 어렵거나 덜 친숙한 은유 표현의 해석에는 좌반구와는 질적으로 다른 활성 패턴을 보이는 우반구의 중/하전두회(middle and inferior frontal gyrus, rMFG/rIFG)가 동원된다고 보고하였다(각 부위의 뇌에서의 위치에 대하여 그림 1을 참조하시오). 즉 은유 표현의 해석은 난이도나 상투성, 친숙도 등이 요인으로 작용하여 뇌의 활성을 조절하는 것으로 볼 수 있다.

3.4. 반어의 신경 기제

또 다른 비유적 표현인 반어(irony)의 연구에서 Eviatar and Just(2006)는 은유와 달리 반어는 화자가 자신이 말한 것을 의미하지 않는다는 것이 명백해야 할 뿐 아니라 해당 발화가 전체 이야기 속에 통합되는 것을 계산할 수 있어야 한다는 점을 지적했다. 그들은 두뇌에 이상이 없는 참가자들에게서 반어 해석 시 축어나 은유 해석 때와 달리 우상측두회와 우중측두회(right superior and middle temporal gyri, rSTG/rMTG)에서 높은 수준의 활성을 관찰하

---

8 Rapp et al.(2004)은 좌하전두회(lIFG)는 의미적 추론 과정에 개입하였을 것이고, 좌측두회(lTG)도 단어의 의미 추론에 기여했을 것으로 보고 있다.

였는데, 이는 담화 속의 흩어진 개체들(entities) 사이에 관계를 구축하여 결속성(coherence)을 계산하는 과정을 나타내는 것이라고 설명하였다. 즉 반어 이해의 신경 활성은 화자가 한 말과 반대로 이해하기 위해서 언어적, 상황적 맥락에 대한 이해가 우선시되고 반어 표현이 여기에 통합되는 과정을 보여주는 것이라고 요약할 수 있다. 다른 한편 Matsui, Nakamura, Utsumi, Sasaki, Koike, Yoshida, Harada, Tanabe, and Sadato(2016)는 반어는 발화의 내용과 운율의 불일치로 인식될 수 있는 것으로써 좌우의 하전두엽(inferior frontal lobe, IFL) 지역이 이러한 인식에 대한 활성을 보인다고 하였다(각 부위의 뇌에서의 위치에 대하여 그림 1을 참조하시오).

3.5. 거짓말의 신경 기제

종종 반어와 병행하여 연구되는 거짓말은 거짓말하는 사람의 믿음을 이해하고, 또 마음의 표상적, 정보적 개념을 이해하는 데 유용한 지표로 여겨진다(Perner 1991:189). 거짓말의 신경적 연구는 주로 어떤 질문에 대해 거짓말로 답하도록 유도하여 그 결과를 관찰하는데, 그러한 경우 양반구의 배외전전두피질(dorsolateral prefrontal cortext, dlPFC)과 복외전전두피질(ventrolateral prefrontal cortex, vlPFC), 전대상피질(anterior cingulate cortex, aCC), 후두정피질(posterior parietal cortex, pPC) 등 실행기능(executive function)과 연관된 지역의 두드러진 활성이 관찰된다(Christ, Van Essen, Watson, Brubaker, and McDermott 2009). Christ et al.(2009)은 이 실행기능에는 거짓 답변을 하면서도 진실을 계속 생각하는 작업기억, 진실된 답변이 튀어나오지 않도록 억누르는 억제력, 진실과 거짓 답변 사이를 오가는 과제 변경 등의 기능이 포함된다고 보았다. 하지만 Yin and Weber(2018)는 실험참가자들에게 거짓말이나 참말을 자유롭게 선택하도록 할 경우에는 거짓말을 통해 얻을 수 있는 보상을 평가하고 이를 위해 인지적 자원을 할당하는 영역들, 즉 꼬리핵(caudate nucleus, CN), 하전두회(IFG), 배외전전두피질(dlPFC), 복내전전두피질(ventromedial prefrontal cortex, vmPFC) 등이 동원된다는 결과를 보고하였다(각 부위의 뇌에서의 위치에 대하여 그림 1을 참조하시오).

이상에서 살펴본 화용적 현상에 동원되는 신경기반에 대한 결과를 바탕으로 하여 다음 절에서는 화자나 청자가 화용적 발화를 생산하거나 이해할 때 뇌에서 일어날 화용론적으로 유의미한 변화에 대하여 논의한다.

4. 신경화용론의 결과 적용

이 절에서는 앞 절의 연구 결과들이 서로 다른 조합으로 다양하게 적용될 만한 세 가지의 발화를 선정하여 이 발화들의 화용적 해석에 동원될 수 있는 가능한 뇌 영역들을 찾아볼 것이다. 3절에서 언급한 뇌 영역들을 여기에서는 괄호 안에 로마자 약자로 표기한다(예: mPFC = medial prefrontal cortex, 내전전두피질).

먼저 위에서 살펴본 (1)의 대화에서 '지금 몇 시지?'라는 발화를 들은 B의 뇌에서 일어나게 될 화용론적으로 유의미한 변화에는 어떤 것이 있을까? (언어적 의사소통의 예이지만 여기에서는 통사, 의미, 음운 분석에 동원되는 전통적인 언어 영역에 대한 논의는 제외한다.)

    (1) A: 지금 몇 시지?

        B: 응? 이제 뭐 좀 먹을까?

A: 그러자.

우선 B에게서는 A의 의도를 파악하기 위하여 마음이론 기제가 작동할 것이다. 이 마음이론 기제는 B로 하여금 발화의 장소와 시간적 환경을 표상하게 하고(TPJ, STS), A의 얼굴, 표정, 제스처 등의 정보를 수집하며(ITG, TPJ, STS, amygdala), 시간과 식사를 관련짓는 기억을 인출하는 한편(TP, mPFC) A의 욕구나 의도 등의 정신적 상태를 추론하는(mPFC, TPJ, STS, aPCC) 뇌 영역들이 활성화됨으로써 A가 평소의 식사 때와 가까운 시간이 되었는지를 궁금해 하고 있음을 추론하게 할 것이다. 또한 B가 A의 질문에 단순히 해당 시간을 알려주지 않은 것은 발화를 ('밥을 먹자'는 제안이나 요청의) 간접화행으로 인식한 것이므로 식사를 하기 위한 준비나 이동 등 운동을 예측하여 계획하는 운동 영역(IPL, pre-SMA) 또한 활성화될 것이라고 예측할 수 있다.

그렇다면 (1)과 다른 화용적 현상을 포함한 발화를 해석할 때는 뇌의 어느 부위가 활성화될지 다음 예를 통해 살펴보자.

(2) 아까 낮에 남편이 참 일찍도 일어나서 부엌을 어슬렁거리는데, 그 모습을 보니까 내 속이 막 부글부글 끓어오르더라.

보통 스스럼없는 사이에서 일어나는 (2)와 같은 발화는 화자가 자신의 남편의 생활양식에 대해 불만을 토로하며 청자로부터 공감을 얻고자 하는 목적을 전달한다. 화자의 이러한 목적과 의도를 파악하기 위하여 청자에게서는 (1)에서와 같이 마음이론 기제가 활성화될 것이다. 이 기제는 대화가 이루어지는 장소 및 시간의 표상(TPJ, STS), 화자의 불만스러운 표정과 제스처 표상(ITG, TPJ, STS, amygdala), 화자가 자신의 남편에 대하여 했던 언급

회상(TP, mPFC), 청자의 공감을 얻으려는 화자의 의도 추론(mPFC, TPJ, STS, aPCC) 등의 기능을 수행할 것이다. 이에 더해 '참 일찍도 일어나서'를 반어적으로 해석하기 위하여 '낮에(즉 늦은 시간에) 일어나는 것'과 '속이 끓는 것' 사이의 인과관계를 이해하고 이것을 맥락으로 하여 해당 발화를 통합하기 위한(rSTG, rMTG) 뇌의 활성이 일어나며, 늦게 일어난 것을 일찍 일어났다고 말하는 반어 특유의 운율에 대한 파악(lIFL, rIFL) 역시 수반되어 '아주 늦게 일어나서'로 해석하게 될 것이다. 그리고 '속이 막 부글부글 끓어오르더라'를 은유적으로 이해하기 위한 뇌영역(lIFG, lMTG, lITG)의 활성 또한 기대할 수 있다.[9]

다음은 밖에 비가 내리고 있다고 생각하여 우산을 들고 나가려는 청자에게 화자가 장난 삼아 하는 거짓말의 예이다.

(3) 날씨 괜찮네.

(3)은 청자가 화자의 말을 믿고 우산을 놓고 밖에 나갔다가 비가 오는 것을 알고 다시 와서 갖고 가게 할 목적으로 생성된 발화라고 가정하자. 이 경우 청자가 (3)을 날씨에 대한 단순한 진술이 아닌 '우산 놓고 가도 돼'라는 의미를 가진 권고의 간접화행으로 이해하려면 화자의 진지한 표정을 표상하는 영역(ITG, TPJ, STS, amygdala), 밤새 내리던 비가 이제는 그쳤으리라고 추론하는 영역(IFG), 날이 개면 우산이 필요 없다는 의미 기억을 표상하는 영역(TP), 자신을 배려하고자 하는 화자의 의도를 추론하는 영역(mPFC,

---

9 '속이 끓는다'는 상투적인 은유 표현이므로 여기에는 Rapp et al.(2004)의 결과를 표기하였다.

TPJ, STS, aPCC) 등 마음이론 기제를 포함한 여러 영역들이 동원될 것이다.

다른 한편 거짓말인 (3)을 발화하는 화자의 입장에서 가능한 신경적 변화를 예상해보면, (청자의 이전의 행위에 대한 되갚음이든 단순히 장난을 즐겁게 여기든) 청자가 나갔다가 돌아왔을 때의 표정을 자신의 행위에 대한 보상으로 여기는 영역(CN, IFG, dlPFC, vmPFC),[10] 청자가 자신의 말을 믿지 않을 경우에 취할 행동이나 늦기 전에 진실을 말할지에 대한 고민에 동원되는 영역들 (dlPFC, vlPFC, aCC, pPC)이 활성화될 것이다. 또한 청자가 이러한 종류의 장난에 반응했던 기억을 회상하거나(TP, mPFC) 청자의 현재의 기분을 살피는(ITG, TPJ, STS, amygdala) 마음이론 기제 또한 활성화하리라고 예상할 수 있다.

이제까지 살펴본 (1)-(3)에서의 화자나 청자의 화용적 처리 과정에 주로 활성화될 영역들을 기능으로 묶어 정리하면 다음과 같다.

> (4) 대화 (1)의 B: 마음이론 기제, 운동 영역
>
> (5) 예문 (2)의 청자: 마음이론 기제, 반어 해석 영역, 은유 해석 영역
>
> (6) 예문 (3)의 청자: 마음이론 기제
>
> (7) 예문 (3)의 화자: 마음이론 기제, 보상 회로, 실행기능

(4)-(7)에 열거된 영역이 모두 화용적 이해에 동원된다고 발표된 것임을 감안할 때, 이 중 어떤 것을 화용적 원리의 신경기반으로 보는 것이 좋을지 다음 절에서 논의해 본다.

---

10 보상과 관련된 신경기반에는 꼬리핵(CN)과 조가비핵(putamen) 등이 포함된 기저핵(basal ganglia)의 여러 지역과 전대상피질(aCC), 안와전전두피질(orbital prefrontal cortex, oPFC) 등 여러 피질 지역이 포함된다(Haber and Knutson 2009).

5. 화용적 원리의 신경 기반에 대한 가설과 논의

화용적 원리는 정의상 모든 화용적 현상에 작동하는 것이므로 이 절에서는 위 (4)-(7) 중 화용적 신경 상관물에 해당될 영역에 대한 세 가지 가설을 설정하여 각각의 타당성을 논할 것이다.

5.1. 가설 1

화용적 해석을 이끄는 보편적 원리에 대한 신경적 기반의 첫 번째 후보로 눈에 띄는 것은 (4)-(7)에서 공통적으로 활성화되는 '마음이론 기제'이다. 3절에서도 언급한 자폐증이나 외상성 뇌손상, 우반구 손상 환자뿐 아니라 조현병 환자에 대한 연구에서도 화용적 손실을 마음이론 손실의 결과로 지목하고 있고(Frith 1992), 최근의 신경기반에 대한 연구에서는 마음이론과 화용적 이해의 신경 기반이 상당히 중복된다는 결과를 내놓은 바 있다(Frank 2018). 또한 Sperber and Wilson(2002)은 화용적 이해 과정이 마음읽기(즉 마음이론)의 하위모듈로서 이 과정에서 적합성 기반의 절차가 직시적 자극(ostensive stimuli)에 자동으로 적용된다고 하였다. 즉 병리학적 연구나 인지신경과학적 연구 등에서 화용적 능력과 마음이론 능력을 아주 밀접한 관계로 보기도 하고, 또 (4)-(7)에서와 같이 항상 작동하는 것으로 보이며, 대화 상대와 협동을 하거나 적합성을 계산하는 인지 과정에서 상대방의 정신적 상태(mental state)를 파악하는 것은 필수적인 일이므로 마음이론 기제를 화용적 원리의 신경기반으로 간주하는 것이 상당히 그럴 듯해 보인다.

하지만 이 가설은 마음이론 기제가 비유 표현 해석이나 간접화행의 의미 파악 등을 주도하는 원리로서 작용한다는 증거가 있어야 성립이 가능하다.

3절에서 살펴보았듯이 마음이론 기제는 스스로의 생각을 모니터링하고 (mPFC), 자신과 타인의 생각을 구별하며(TPJ), 얼굴을 인식하는(ITG) 등 각각 의 기능을 하는 여러 뇌 부위가 회로처럼 작용하여 행동과 정신적 상태를 연결 짓는 기능으로 실현되는 것이므로 이 체계의 기능부전이 마음이론 능력의 장애로 나타나고, 마음이론 능력의 손실이 화용적 기능 상실에 영향을 준다는 것은 많은 연구를 통해 밝혀진 바 있다. 하지만 이 사실이 마음이론 기제가 화용적 해석의 신경기반으로 작용했다는 직접적이며 경험적인 증거 가 될 수는 없다. 왜냐하면 Bosco, Tirassa, and Gabbatore(2018)가 지적하듯 이 대부분의 연구에서 마음이론 능력은 틀린 믿음 과제를 통해 측정하고 화용적 능력은 화용적 현상 이해하기 과제를 통해 측정하기 때문에 각각의 독립적인 능력을 독립적인 방식으로 측정한 결과를 어느 정도까지 융합할 수 있을지는 미지수다. 그리고 이러한 이유로 마음이론 테스트는 통과하지만 반어 테스트는 통과하지 못하거나(Bosco and Gabbatore 2017) 마음이론 테스트 를 다 통과하지는 못하지만 은유 테스트는 통과하는 결과가 나오기도 하는 것이다(Langdon, Davies, and Coltheart 2002). 이러한 맥락에서 Frank(2018)가 내놓은 두 능력 간의 중복되는 신경기반에 대한 결과 또한 마음이론 능력이 화용적 수행을 제어하거나 이끈다는 증거가 될 수는 없다. 더욱이 Sperber and Wilson(2002)도 적합성적 절차가 개입하여 화용적 이해가 작동된다고 설명하지 마음이론 기제 자체가 화용적 해석의 원리로 작동한다고 보지는 않았다. 따라서 화용적 원리가 마음이론 기제를 통해 실현된다는 가설의 근거는 불충분한 것으로 보인다.

5.2. 가설 2

두 번째 가설은 (4)-(7)에서 열거된 모든 활성 영역들의 합집합을 화용적 원리의 신경기반으로 보는 것이다. 즉 마음이론 기제는 물론이고 운동 영역, 반어 해석 영역, 은유 해석 영역, 보상 회로, 실행기능 영역들 전부를 화용적 원리의 신경기반으로 가정하게 되면 마음읽기와 더불어 어떤 화용적 의미의 해석도 관장할 수 있을 것이므로 첫 번째 가설의 문제가 해결될 것이다.

그러나 이 모든 영역들 전체를 화용적 원리의 신경기반으로 볼 경우의 문제는 언어적 의사소통에 대한 원리와 신경생리학적 결과 사이에 충돌이 일어나리라는 것이다. 왜냐하면 화용적 원리는 화용적 해석을 위한 모든 상황에서 언제나 작동할 것으로 기대되는 것이기 때문에 가령 (1), (3)에서와 같이 비유적 표현이 없는 경우에도 비유적 표현을 해석하는 영역을 포함한 모든 영역이 활성화되고 (2)에서와 같이 화자가 거짓말을 하지 않을 때도 거짓을 감추기 위한 실행기능을 포함한 모든 영역이 활성화된다고 가정해야 하기 때문이다. 즉 각 활성 부위들의 합집합을 화용적 원리라고 가정하면 이 신경망 안의 모든 부위가 동시에 활성화될 필요도 없고 활성화되고 있지 않아도 언제나 활성화된다고 말해야 하는 신경생리학적으로 불가능한 가정을 하게 된다는 뜻이다. 따라서 화용적 수행에 포함되는 모든 부위를 화용적 원리가 실현되는 신경기반으로 보는 가설도 그럴 듯 해 보이지 않는다. 실제로 Reyes-Aguilar, Valles-Capetillo, and Giordano(2018)는 화행, 은유, 숙어, 반어 등의 화용적 현상에 대한 48개의 개별 연구를 종합하여 메타분석을 실시한 후 이러한 화용적 언어를 이해하는 데는 좌우반구의 전두와 측두 영역(BA 44, 45, 47, 21, 22) 및 내전전두피질(mPFC) 등이 동원된다는 결과를 얻어 이를 "화용적 언어 신경망(pragmatic language network)"이라고 명명하였는데, 이는 개별 화용적 현상의 처리에 의한 활성 부위들의 합집합에 해당하는 것이다. 하지만 Reyes-Aguilar et al.(2018)이 설명하는 "화용적 언어 신경망"의 작동 방식은 어떤 화용적 형식(화행, 은유 등)을 해석하느냐에 따라 신경망 내의 다양한 부위들이 선택적으로 동원되는 것이라고 하여 이 신경망 전체가 화용적 원리와 같은 역할을 한다고 보지 않았다. 이는 화용적 처리를 담당하는 모든 부위의 합집합이 화용적 원리를 실현하는 신경기반이 될 수 없다는 것을 뒷받침한다고 할 수 있다.

5.3. 가설 3

마지막 세 번째 가설은 화용적 원리의 신경기반이 존재하지 않을 것이라고 가정하는 것이다. 왜냐하면 첫째 가설에서처럼 어느 한 기제를 특정하면 기능상의 문제가 발생하고 두 번째 가설에서처럼 모든 영역을 포함시키면 신경생리학적으로 불가능한 결과를 낳기 때문에 아예 존재하지 않을 수 있다고 가정하는 것이다. 이 가설의 정당성을 뒷받침하는 첫 번째 근거는 기능적 뇌 영상 기술을 이용한 어떠한 연구에서도 (1)-(3)과 같은 화용적 발화의 해석에 항상 활성화되는 영역이나 회로의 존재에 대한 논의가 없다는 데에 있다. 협동의 원리나 격률의 준수는 대화함축의 존재와 계산에 꼭 필요하고, 적합성의 추정은 함축의미를 알아내는 데는 물론 계산 절차를 언제 멈출지를 결정하는 역할까지도 한다. 정신활동은 반드시 물리적 신경활동을 동반하게 되어있으므로 화용적 원리의 신경회로가 존재한다면 자연스러운 대화를 처리할 때나 인위적 자료를 처리할 때나 가리지 않고, 또 '속이 끓는다'처럼 맥락이 없어도 이해되거나 '남편이 일찍도 일어나서'처럼 맥락이 있어야 이해 가능한 모든 경우에 활성화될 것이 틀림없다. 자신이나 타인의 생각을

파악할 때도, 은유나 반어를 이해할 때도, 그 활성화되는 장소는 달라도 각
각의 화용적 현상을 이끄는 화용적 원리는 반드시 물리적 신경활동을 동반
할 것이다. 하지만 이에 대한 보고가 없다는 사실은 그 존재에 대해 의문을
던지는 근거가 될 수 있다고 주장하고자 한다. 부재에 대한 증명도 불가능하
지만 존재에 대한 보고도 없으므로 존재의 증거가 나오기까지는 부재 가능
성의 주장이 유효할 수 있기 때문이다.

또 다른 근거는 특정 화용적 현상과 특정 뇌 부위를 연결 짓는 신경화용
론의 연구 전통에서 찾을 수 있다. 예를 들어 우반구 손상 환자가 비유적
표현을 지나치게 축어적으로 해석할 때 그 원인을 억제력을 담당하는 전두
엽 부위의 기능적 손실에서 찾는다거나 외상성 뇌 손상 환자가 대화에 방향
이 없이 여러 주제를 옮겨 다닐 때, 혹은 자폐 아동이 문장을 전체 맥락에서
해석하는 데 어려움을 느낄 때 전전두엽의 기능 부전을 그 원인으로 지목하
는 등의 일은 신경화용론적 연구에서 통상적으로 해오고 있고 또 매우 자연
스러운 일로 여겨진다. 하지만 어느 연구에서도 이러한 화용적 수행의 문제
가 협동의 원리나 적합성 원리에 손상을 입었기 때문이라고 추정하지는 않
는다. 더욱이 만약 화용적 원리가 몇몇 뇌 영역의 기능에 의존한다고 가정한
다면 개인마다 화용적 원리를 담당하는 뇌 부위가 다르다거나 화용적 원리
가 뇌 부위의 여기저기를 옮겨 다닌다고 주장해야 할 수도 있을 것이다.
예를 들어, 어떤 이가 비유적 해석에 어려움을 겪게 된 이유가 전두엽 부위
의 신경적 손실로 밝혀졌다면 그의 화용적 원리의 주요 신경기반은 전두엽
에 있었다고 해야 할 것이고, 또 어떤 이가 결속성 있는 담화를 말하지 못하
게 된 이유가 전전두엽의 신경적 손실로 밝혀졌다면 그의 화용적 원리의
주요 신경기반은 전전두엽에 있었다고 봐야 할 것이기 때문이다. 3절에서
살펴보았듯이 특정 화용적 현상을 처리하기 위하여 나름대로의 기능과 역

할을 담당하는 두뇌의 다양한 부위가 동원되는 것은 분명한 사실이다. 하지만 화용적 수행의 장애를 고차원적 원리가 아닌 특정 뇌 부위와 연관 짓는 신경화용론의 연구 전통은 화용적 원리 자체를 담당하는 신경기반이 따로 존재하지 않는다는 증거가 될 수 있다는 것이다.

요컨대 마음이론 기제는 화용적 원리로 보기에 충분한 증거가 뒷받침되지 못하고, (4)~(7)의 모든 영역을 화용적 원리의 신경기반으로 보는 것은 신경생리학적으로 불가능한 가정이므로 본고에서는 신경화용론의 연구에서 이에 대한 논의가 전혀 없다는 점과 화용적 수행의 문제를 뇌의 해부학적인 문제로 삼는 연구 경향 등을 근거로 들어 협동의 원리나 적합성 원리와 같은 화용적 원리를 담당하는 신경기반은 존재하지 않을 수 있다는 가능성을 제기하였다.

6. 결론

본고는 뇌의 메커니즘에 대한 이해 없이는 화용적 현상을 근본적으로 설명하기 어렵다는 데에서 출발하여 지금까지 신경화용론의 연구에서 시도한 적 없는 화용적 원리의 신경기반을 추정해 보는 것을 목적으로 하였다. 우선 지난 수십 년 간 신경화용론의 기능적 뇌 영상 연구에서 화용적 현상에 동원된다고 발표된 뇌 영역들의 결과를 취합하여 이중 어떤 영역이 화용적 의미의 해석이나 생산을 이끄는 화용적 원리의 신경기반이 될지 알아보기 위하여 이 결과를 다양한 종류의 발화에 적용하여 보았다. 화용적 처리에 동원될 수 있는 가능한 뇌 영역들을 정리한 결과 마음이론 기제가 모든 발화에 공통적으로 동원되기도 하고 또 화용적 수행에 지대한 영향을 미치는 것이 사실이나 화용적 처리를 관장하는 원리로서 작용한다는 증거는 부족하다고 보았다. 또 다른 후보는 마음이론 기제와 더불어 화용적 수행에 동원될 모든 영역들의 모음으로 삼았는데, 이는 신경생리학적으로 불가능한 가정이므로 적절하지 않다고 보았다. 따라서 마지막으로 화용적 원리의 신경기반은 애초에 없는 것이라고 가정하였다. 이제까지의 신경화용론 연구에서 은유, 간접화행, 관련성 함축의미(relevance implicature) 등 개별적인 화용적 현상에 대한 연구 외에 화용적 원리 자체의 신경기반에 대한 논의가 전혀 없다는 점과 화용적 수행의 문제를 뇌의 해부학적인 문제로 삼는 연구 경향, 그리고 몇몇 부위를 화용적 원리의 신경기반으로 여길 경우에 발생할 수 있는 문제 등을 근거로 들어 화용적 원리의 신경기반은 없다고 주장하였다.

만약 화용적 원리의 신경상관물이 존재하지 않으면 화용적 의미의 파악이 어떻게 가능할까? 이는 향후의 연구과제로서 나는 추상적인 원리가 아닌 마음이론 기제를 비롯한 각주 5에서 언급한 실행기능(executive function)과 중앙적 결속성(central coherence), 그리고 기본 신경망(default network) 등 인간의 일반적 인지작용의 신경기반이 모두 동원될 것이며, 또한 유아기부터 피질 곳곳에 저장된 사회적 상호작용의 다양성이 화용적 해석의 근거가 된다고 제안할 것이다. 이러한 연구의 결과는 화용적 발달이 다른 언어적 능력에 비해 매우 늦게 완성되는 이유와 화용적 능력이 뇌 손상으로 인해 영향을 받는 이유를 설명하게 될 것이다.

Works Cited

Bambini, Valentina, and Bruno G. Bara. 2012. Neuropragmatics. In Jef Verschueren and Jan-Ola Östman (eds.), *Handbook of Pragmatics Online*, 1-21. Amsterdam: Benjamins.

Bara, Bruno G., and Angela Ciaramidaro. 2010. Intentions in the brain. *Italian Journal of Linguistics/Rivista di Linguistica* 22, 89-105.

Baron-Cohen, Simon, Alan Leslie, and Uta Frith. 1985. Does the autistic child have a "theory of mind"? *Cognition* 21, 37-46.

Bosco, Francesca, and Ilaria Gabbatore. 2017. Sincere, deceitful, and ironic communicative acts and the role of the theory of mind in childhood. *Frontiers in Psychology*. 8. doi.10.3389/fpsyg.2017.00021

Bosco, Francesca, Maurizio Tirassa, and Ilaria Gabbatore. 2018. Why pragmatics and theory of mind do not (completely) overlap. *Frontiers in Psychology* 13. doi.10.3389/fpsyg.2018.01453

Bottini, Gabriella, Rhiannon Corcoran, Roberto Sterzi, Eraldo Paulesu, Pietro Schenone, Pina Scarpa, Richard Frackowiak, and Christopher D. Frith. 1994. The role of the right hemisphere in the interpretation of figurative aspects of language: A positron emission tomography activation study. *Brain* 117, 1241-1253.

Champagne-Lavau, Maud, and Yves Joanette. 2009. Pragmatics, theory of mind and executive functions after a right-hemisphere lesion: Different patterns of deficits. *Journal of Neurolinguistics* 22(5), 413-426.

Christ, Shawn, David Van Essen, Jason Watson, Lindsay Brubaker, and Kathleen McDermott. 2009. The contributions of prefrontal cortex and executive control to deception: Evidence from activation likelihood estimate meta-analyses. *Cerebral Cortex* 19(7), 1557-1566.

Conway, Bevil. 2018. The organization and operation of inferior temporal cortex. *Annual Review of Vision Science* 15(4), 381-402. doi.10.1146/annurev-vision

-091517-034202

Critchley, Macdonald. 1962. Speech and speech-loss in relation to duality of the brain. In Vernon B. Mountcastle (ed.), *Interhemispheric Relations and Cerebral Dominance*, 208-213. Baltimore: Johns Hopkins University Press.

Damasio, Antonio R. 2000. *Descartes' Error: Emotion, Reason, and the Human Brain*. New York: Quill.

Delis, Dean, Wendy Wapner, Howard Gardner, and James Moses. 1983. The contribution of the right hemisphere to the organization of paragraphs. *Cortex: A Journal Devoted to the Study of the Nervous System and Behavior* 19(1), 43-50. doi.org/10.1016/S0010-9452(83)80049-5

Edelman, Gerald. 1992. *Bright Air, Brilliant Fire: On the Matter of the Mind*. Basic Books.

Eisenson, Jon. 1962. Language and intellectual modifications associated with right cerebral damage. *Language and Speech* 5, 49-53.

Euston, David, Aaron Gruber, and Bruce McNaughton. 2012. The role of medial prefrontal cortex in memory and decision making. *Neuron* 76(6), 1057-1070. doi.10.1016/j.neuron.2012.12.002

Eviatar, Zohar, and Marcel Adam Just. 2006. Brain correlates of discourse processing: An fMRI investigation of irony and conventional metaphor comprehension. *Neuropsychologia* 44(12), 2348-2359.

Frank, Chiyoko Kobayashi. 2018. Reviving pragmatic theory of theory of mind. *AIMS Neuroscience* 5(2), 116-131. doi.10.3934/Neuroscience.2018.2.116

Frith, Christopher D. 1992. *The Cognitive Neuropsychology of Schizophrenia*. Lawrence Erlbaum Associates.

Gallagher, Helen, and Christopher D. Frith. 2003. Functional imaging of 'theory of mind'. *Trends in Cognitive Sciences* 7(2), 77-83.

Grice, Herbert Paul. 1975. Logic and conversation. In Peter Cole and Jerry Morgan (eds.), *Syntax and Semantics*, Vol. 3, 41-58. New York: Academic Press.

Haber, Suzanne, and Brian Knutson. 2009. The reward circuit: Linking primate anatomy and human imaging. *Neuropsychopharmacology* 35, 4-26.

Hagoort, Peter, and Jos van Berkum. 2007. Beyond the sentence given. *Philosophical*

Transactions of the Royal Society B: Biological Sciences 362, 801–811.

Jang, Gijeong, Shin-ae Yoon, Sung-Eun Lee, Haeil Park, Joohan Kim, Jeong Hoon Ko, and Hae-Jeong Park. 2013. Everyday conversation requires cognitive inference: Neural bases of comprehending implicated meanings in conversations. *NeuroImage* 81, 61–72.

Joanette, Yves, and Pierre Goulet. 1994. Right hemisphere and verbal communication: Conceptual, methodological, and clinical issues. *Clinical Aphasiology* 22, 1–23.

Kandel, Eric, James Schwartz, Thomas Jessell, Steven Siegelbaum, and A. J. Hudspeth. (eds.) 2013. *Principles of Neural Science* 5th ed. McGraw Hill Professional.

Kaplan, Joan, H. Hiram Brownell, Janet Jacobs, and Howard Gardner. 1990. The effects of right hemisphere damage on the pragmatic interpretation of conversational remarks. *Brain and Language* 38(2), 315–333. doi.org/10.1016/0093-934X(90)90 117-Y

Langdon, Robyn, Martin Davies, and Max Coltheart. 2002. Understanding minds and understanding communicated meanings in schizophrenia. *Mind and Language* 17, 68–104. doi.10.1111/1468-0017.00190

Martin, Ingerith, and Skye McDonald. 2003. Weak coherence, no theory of mind, or executive dysfunction? Solving the puzzle of pragmatic language disorders. *Brain and Language* 85, 451–466.

Matsui, Tomoko, Tagiru Nakamura, Akira Utsumi, Akihiro Sasaki, Takahiko Koike, Yumiko Yoshida, Tokiko Harada, Hiroki Tanabe, and Norihiro Sadato. 2016. The role of prosody and context in sarcasm comprehension: Behavioral and fMRI evidence. *Neuropsychologia* 87, 74–84.

Pelphrey, Kevin, James Morris, and Gregory McCarthy. 2004. Grasping the intentions of others: the perceived intentionality of an action influences activity in the superior temporal sulcus during social perception. *Journal of Cognitive Neuroscience* 16(10), 1706–1716. doi.10.1162/0898929042947900

Perner, Josef. 1991. *Understanding the Representational Mind*. Cambridge, MA: MIT Press.

Premack, David, and Guy Woodruff. 1978. Does the chimpanzee have a theory of mind? *The Behavioral and Brain Sciences* 4, 515–526.

Quesque, Francois, and Marcel Brass. 2019. The role of the temporoparietal junction in self–other distinction. *Brain Topography* 32, 943–955.

Rapp, Alexander, Dirk Leube, Michael Erb, Wolfgang Grodd, and Tilo Kircher. 2004. Neural correlates of metaphor processing. *Cognitive Brain Research* 20, 395–402.

Reyes–Aguilar, Azalea, Elizabeth Valles–Capetillo, and Magda Giordano. 2018. A quantitative meta–analysis of neuroimaging studies of pragmatic language comprehension: In search of a universal neural substrate. *Neuroscience* 395, 60–88.

Schmidt, Gwenda, and Carol Seger. 2009. Neural correlates of metaphor processing: The roles of figurativeness, familiarity and difficulty. *Brain and Cognition* 71, 375–386.

Shaw, Philip, Emma Lawrence, Claire Radbourne, Jessica Bramham, Charles Polkey, and Anthony David. 2004. The impact of early and late damage to the human amygdala on 'theory of mind' reasoning. *Brain* 127(7), 1535–1548. doi.10.1093/brain/awh168

Sperber, Dan, and Deirdre Wilson. 1986. *Relevance: Communication and Cognition.* Oxford: Basil Blackwell.

Sperber, Dan, and Deirdre Wilson. 2002. Pragmatics, modularity, and mind–reading. *Mind and Language* 17, 3–23.

van Ackeren, Markus, Daniel Casasanto, Harold Bekkering, Peter Hagoort, and Shirley–Ann Rueschemeyer. 2012. Pragmatics in action: Indirect requests engage theory of mind areas and the cortical motor network. *Journal of Cognitive Neuroscience* 24(11), 2237–2247.

Winner, Ellen, and Howard Gardner. 1977. The comprehension of metaphors in brain damaged patients. *Brain* 100, 717–729.

Wimmer, Heinz, and Josef Perner. 1983. Beliefs about beliefs: Representation and constraining function of wrong beliefs in young children's understanding of deception. *Cognition* 13(1), 103–128.

Yin, Lijun, and Bernd Weber. 2018. I lie, why don't you: Neural mechanisms of individual differences in self-serving lying. *Human Brain Mapping* 40(4). Wiley Online Library. doi.org/10.1002/hbm.24432

저자 소개 (논문 게재 순)

김형민

오스트리아 잘츠부르크(Salzburg)대학교 철학박사

숭실대학교 독어독문학과 교수

(현재) 서강대학교 유럽문화학과 교수

신승용

서강대학교 박사

서강대학교 대우전임강사

이화여자대학교 BK21 연구교수

(현재) 영남대학교 국어교육과 교수

정수정

독일 라이프치히대학교 박사

서울대학교 강사

(현재) 충북대학교 독일언어문화학과 교수

김광섭

미국 메릴랜드대학교(University of Maryland, College Park) 언어학 박사

한국생성문법학회장

한국외대 통번역대학장

(현재) 한국외국어대학교 영어통번역학부 교수

연재훈

런던대학교 철학(언어학) 박사

런던대학교 SOAS 한국학과 교수

(현재) 런던대학교 SOAS 명예교수, 한국학중앙연구원 초빙교수

김지영

서강대학교 대학원 영어영문학과 박사

미국 커네티컷 주립대학교(University of Connecticut) 심리학과 박사 후 연구원

서울시립대학교 강의전담객원교수

(현재) 서강대학교 언어정보연구소 책임연구원

호모 로퀜스 정체 밝히기

초판 1쇄 인쇄 2022년 3월 5일
초판 1쇄 발행 2022년 3월 15일

지은이 김형민 신승용 정수정 김광섭 연재훈 김지영
펴낸이 이대현

책임편집 강윤경 | **편집** 이태곤 권분옥 문선희 임애정
디자인 안혜진 최선주 이경진 | **마케팅** 박태훈 안현진
펴낸곳 도서출판 역락 | **등록** 1999년 4월 19일 제303-2002-000014호
주소 서울시 서초구 동광로46길 6-6 문창빌딩 2층(우06589)
전화 02-3409-2060(편집부), 2058(영업부) | **팩스** 02-3409-2059
전자우편 youkrack@hanmail.net | **홈페이지** www.youkrackbooks.com

ISBN 979-11-6742-292-7 94700
      979-11-85530-81-9 (세트)